EVALUATING SUCCESS OF A Y2000 PROJECT

Evaluating Success of a Y2000 Project

Howard Rubin and Brian Robbins

with foreword by Richard Nolan, Harvard Business School, and comment by Paul Strassmann, Software Testing Assurance Corporation

IEP

The Information Economics Press
NEW CANAAN, CONNECTICUT
1998

Production Coordination and Design: David Shaw, Belm Design
Printing: Braun-Brumfield

Order from:
THE INFORMATION ECONOMICS PRESS / BOOKMASTERS
Distribution Center, 1444 US Route 42, Mansfield, Ohio,
Phone 800-800-0448; Fax: 419-281-6883
E-mail: bkmaster@worldnet.att.net
Internet: http://www.bookmasters.com/marktplc/orderfrm.htm

Printed in the United States of America
1 2 3 4 5 6 7 8 9 10

Rubin, Howard and Robbins, Brian
Evaluating Success of a Y2000 Project
1. Strategic Planning   2. Information Technology
3. Business Management   I. Title
1998   658.4
Library of Congress Catalog Card Number 98-07637
ISBN 0-9620413-7-8

TABLE OF CONTENTS

Table of Contents   *v*

About the Authors   *vi*

Foreword   *vii*

Introduction   1

Interpreting Your Score   4

QuickSTATus Test   5

Drill-Down Questions   6

Robbins-Rubin Year 2000 Performance Indices   16

Business Network Analysis   21

What to Do Next   23

Resources   25

Afterword   35

Year 2000 Survey Results   42

Comments About Y2000 Test Certification   47

A Y2000 Testing Certification Standard   50

For More Information   73

About the Authors

Dr. Howard A. Rubin

DR. HOWARD RUBIN is a tenured Full Professor and Chair of the Department of Computer Science at Hunter College of the City University of New York; the CEO of Rubin Systems, Inc.; a Faculty Affiliate of Cap Gemini America and the Meta Group; and a former Nolan Norton Research Fellow. He is the Software Metrics Area Editor for *IEEE Computer* and the Editor of Cutter Information's *IT Metrics Strategies*. He has published two software engineering books on metrics and quality, and has produced more than 50 papers which have appeared in refereed academic journals, professional conference proceedings, and trade publications. In 1997, *Industry Week* named Dr. Rubin as one of the top 50 "R&D Stars to Watch... an individual whose achievements are shaping the future of our industrial culture and America's technology policy" as a result of his bringing the IT workforce shortage to national attention in his role as Chair of the National Task Force on Software Quality and Productivity.

Brian D. Robbins

BRIAN ROBBINS is a Senior Vice President at Chase Manhattan Bank and is responsible for managing Chase's Enterprise Year 2000 Program Office. In this role, he has helped establish a global strategy for managing all aspects of the bank's Year 2000 program. Prior to joining Chase, he was directly involved with large systems design and integration efforts, primarily with Andersen Consulting. He has a BS from Georgetown University and a MBA from the University of Notre Dame.

FOREWORD

© 1998 *Richard Nolan, Harvard Business School*

ONLY THE IT community could come up with an acronym like Y2K to take a straightforward problem and make it so obtuse as to cloud its importance and impact on companies. Y2K stands for the Year 2000 problem. The problem simply is that over the past 30 years computer programmers hard coded dates into hardware and software programs using only 2 digits rather than 4. So when the clock strikes 12:00 on the night of December 31, 1999, many computer programs of companies will roll over from 99 to 00 rather than from 1999 to 2000. Well, so what?

Y2K is a ticking time bomb for every company, and as the clock ticks toward the year 2000 time is fast running out to defuse the bomb. CEOs need to seize leadership in sizing the company's Y2K problem, and mobilize action to correct it. Boards need to conduct oversight to ensure progress is being made to reduce the Y2K business risk exposure to acceptable levels.

SOME ADVICE ON SIZING YOUR COMPANY'S PROBLEM

IN SIZING the problem, there are six types of computer systems that need to be assessed for data rollover failure:
- Home-grown transaction processing systems
- Purchased and outsourced vendor systems
- Home-grown PC-based systems
- Interorganizational systems with suppliers, customers, and competitors
- Government or regulatory systems that are used
- Systems embedded in hardware and software such as systems in process control machinery, ATMs, and building security.

Each type of system has unique characteristics which require different approaches to correct the date rollover failure.

Home-Grown Systems

Home-grown transaction systems are the most problematic to fix. Many of the home-grown systems are mission-critical systems of companies such as loan programs, plant scheduling, inventory management, and order processing that were written in what now seems to be archaic programming languages such as COBOL, FORTRAN, and even BAL (IBM's Basic Assembler Language for the IBM 360 series). Virtually every medium to large company has some of these programs in their applications portfolios. These programs are nightmares to maintain, enhance, and keep running, but they have just kept working. Most of the programmers who developed the code are long retired; few of these programmers documented their programs very well, nor were they required to. Over the years, new generations of programmers have been able to graft new technologies such as PCs onto these programs, or add features such as graphic oriented report generators. In past examinations of these kinds of systems, they are often replete with what is called dead code: code that is not used anymore and is disabled in the program. Dead code comes to life every once in awhile to make maintenance and debugging of logic even more difficult.

Attempts to reconstruct the logic flows of these programs is extremely difficult and slow going. Even once done, the flowcharts end up looking like spaghetti thrown against the wall – thus, the term spaghetti code.

Costs to make legacy systems Year 2000 compliant have been estimated to be up to $6 per line of code. Typically medium-sized companies will have 5,000 to 10,000 of these types of programs in their portfolios averaging 1,500 to 2,000 lines of code. The collection of programs around main functions such as supply chain logistics can run into millions of lines of code. Just to fix the legacy systems runs in the tens of millions dollars.

AT&T estimates from $500 – $700 million to fix their Y2K problem; EDS and FedEx estimate $500 million. To put the issue into a national perspective, the estimated costs for US companies to correct the Y2K problem exceeds $200 billion.

Several years ago, COBOL programmers were considered obsolete and a dying breed. Today, COBOL programmers are one of the most sought after skills in the IT profession – right up there with highly sought after C++ and Java programmers. Increasingly companies are luring long retired COBOL programmers out of retirement. In one instance, a company set up a virtual office in the nursing home residence for one of its retired COBOL programmers who was the main developer of a 25-year old system.

Making a company's IT systems Year 2000 compliant is consuming major resources in firms such as Andersen Consulting, IBM Global Consulting, and Keane. Not only is it extremely difficult to access outside resources to work on the problem, but the daily rates of these resources are continually being pushed up due to the rapidly increasing demand for the scarce talent. If you are looking for consulting help today, you need to be doubly vigilant about the quality of the consulting team being proposed by the vendor.

While there is an emerging set of tools to identify date problems in legacy programs, the tools are just that – tools. Even when the tools are applied, a lot of hard work is required to define the logic. Often, the inability to completely reconstruct program logic – replete with spaghetti code – forces scrapping the program and redeveloping a new one. The overall problem is so complex that for the few companies that got a head start in correcting their Year 2000 problem, some have been able to turn their advantage into a business opportunity.

For those companies that do not have an outsourcing alternative for their legacy mission-critical systems, up to a third of the programs in their application portfolios may be unsalvageable and require replacement. With average development times for major mainframe systems averaging over four years, replacing the systems with new ones hardly seems a viable solution!

Purchased and Outsourced Systems

For home-grown mission-critical systems, the company at least has control over the systems; this is not true for purchased and outsourced mission-critical systems. For purchased and outsourced systems, other specialized firms keep the programs running. These systems include not only the business applications that we are most familiar with, such as payroll, general ledger, and materials requirements planning, but also the software that is necessary to make the computer hardware run. These applications are known as systems software and include the operating system, data base programs, the programming language itself, and various support utilities.

Where a mission-critical system is outsourced or purchased an extremely complex situation exists. For example, assume a basic general ledger system. Most general ledger systems are purchased. The vendor (or contractor) makes specific modifications to the program for your company. Given the Y2K compliant impact of the vendor's overall business, the vendor will first dedicate their programming resources to the standard version of the program. Any company that had specific modifications made to the program is down on the vendor's list of priorities for making Y2K changes. For the company to allocate its own resources to fix the problem, the programmers first have to locate the program source code. In all likelihood the source code of the program is not readily available; and even if it is the code probably has some spaghetti code in it. These kinds of projects can become bottomless sink holes resulting in inefficient resource use.

One of the most significant issues will be dealing with smaller software vendors. Some of these vendors do not have the resources to retroactively make their licensed software Year 2000 compliant, and they know it. Some of these vendors are ignoring the problem, and will simply go out of business if hit with Year 2000 liability lawsuits.

With these formidable challenges, where should a company begin? Letters should be sent to all software vendors of the company requesting Year 2000 certification. While this is start, it is not enough. Already a number of vendors that have certified their software as Year 2000 compliant have been forced to retract their certifications after more rigorous testing by their customers has revealed undetected date problems.

Where possible use one of the Y2K tools to go through the code of each program and identify the number of date changes that are required. Check to make sure that the vendor found all the incidents that you have. Many of these tools are quite good, and they give you a basis to make sure that your vendor is approaching the date problem in an appropriate way. However, the tools may not catch all of the places where date change logic may be troublesome. Accordingly, a test facility is also required whereby the program is tested as if the date had just rolled over to the year 2000. Testing costs are expensive, making up about one-half of the total cost of correcting the date problem, but you never can be sure an errant program is fixed until an actual test is made under real conditions.

There are an increasing number of clever ways emerging to resolve date change problems – from simply increasing the number of digits, to using logic to trap the roll over to the year 2000 and applying software patches to deal with the problem. Depending on the type of program, these alternatives can have wide ranges in costs. Here is where a good Y2K consultant can be of great value.

PC-Based Systems

Since the mid-1980s, PC-based applications have been built by people all over a company. A typical company has thousands of these systems. With the advent of client/server and Internet technologies, many of these systems have been integrated into various networks.

While the first Y2K priority is to launch a program for mission critical systems, the second priority is to launch a program to round up the PC-based systems that may have a Y2K problem. One CEO used a rather straightforward approach. He asked that disks for all such programs be submitted to the Y2K program office for checking and fixing, if necessary. He also announced that if any such programs not submitted brought down the company's 24 × 7 × 52 (i.e., their continuous operation data center) with the rollover in date, everyone up to the Executive Vice President of the functional area will be asked to look for new jobs. He is quite serious about this, and a strong message from the top is important to overcome inertia that exists in most organizations to take the PC-based system Y2K problem seriously.

Interorganizational Systems

There are so many interorganizational computer systems among companies today that the Y2K problem will extend far beyond the boundaries of the individual company. (Many of these interorganizational systems have been extended to the Internet (extranet systems) adding additional levels of complexity to the Y2K problem.) For example, if your suppliers are accessing your production scheduling systems for shipping supplies and parts and your systems are not Year 2000 compliant, they could suffer business losses caused by you.

Worse yet, your customers might be dependent on your computer systems that may experience failure. The risks of interorganizational systems not working because one party does not make their systems Year 2000 compliant even though the other party does is very high.

Obviously, the first step is to identify interorganizational systems. The second step is to meet with all the parties to discuss the problem, approaches to fixing, milestones for monitoring progress, and a joint test program. The test program of multiple parties is probably the most difficult, as well as working out the sharing of the costs to fix problems that are discovered. For example, a common problem arises when one party has a serious problem with spaghetti code requiring expensive rewrite of programs, yet the value of the interorganizational systems are much higher to the other parties. There are not straightforward answers here, but the sooner the companies address their Y2K interorganizational system problems, the sooner teams from the companies can begin working, and the more likely a satisfactory outcome becomes.

The reach and scope of interorganizational systems and extranets with Y2K problems is probably where most of the expensive lawsuits will reside.

Government and Regulatory Systems

Every company has interactions with the government and various regulatory agencies. The Y2K problem is relevant to many of these interactions from the obvious ones involving interorganizational systems to the less obvious ones involving contractual payments, regulatory reporting, and taxes.

The federal government recently appointed a person to head up the Y2K initiative, and she immediately increased the estimate to fix the problem from $2.8 billion to $3.8 billion. Congressman Steven Horn has graded the various agencies on their programs for fixing the Y2K problem, and, for the most part, low grades were given with the exception of the Social Security Administration and the Federal Reserve. Here a company's Y2K program should assess the interactions with the various federal and state governments and regulatory agencies and attempt to anticipate problems. Some of the information on the government's progress and status of Y2K programs is in the public domain.

Regulated organizations may find regulators going beyond their own internal Y2K problems. For example, banks may find regulators going over major loans in the bank's loan portfolio to determine whether there is exposure to defaults because of a debtor's difficulty in becoming Year 2000 compliant.

The Office of Thrift Supervision (OTS) has issued a Year 2000 compliance off-site examination procedure. As reported in *The Wall Street Journal* (October 23, 1997, p. A4), the Securities and Exchange Commission has "told companies and mutual funds they must keep investors informed about the costs of adopting computer systems to handle the change to the Year 2000."

Embedded Systems

Embedded systems are everywhere due to cheaper and cheaper computers on a chip. The power of an IBM PC that cost $3,000 in 1982 is available today for less than $3. So while PCs have remained about the same in price and increased about 500 times in power, a whole other set of lesser powered computer chips have been embedded in every product conceivable from process control equipment to building security systems. Again embedded systems are tricky to identify and nail down. For example, every time a PC powered with a particular chip older than 1986 is booted up after the Year 2000, it will roll over the year 2000 to 1986. An inventory must be made of these systems in the company, and a determination made of risk of a disruptive Y2K problem.

LAUNCHING TO FIX THE Y2K PROBLEM

FIRST YOU have to get your company's attention; second, you need to keep the company's attention until the problem is fixed. Getting appropriate attention comes from the very top beginning with the CEO taking charge to alert the company to the importance and urgency of taking action.

At a minimum, the audit committees of boards need to add Y2K oversight to their agendas, and periodically report to the whole board on progress. Better yet, a board-level y2k committee is an effective way to make a statement to the organization as well as to other constituencies such as shareholders about the importance of the y2k problem and getting it fixed. Board-level committees are unconstrained in ensuring adequate sizing of the y2k problem, as well as motivated to influence the appropriation of necessary resources for fixing the problem.

Funding and Staffing are Essential

My experience is that the majority of companies are underestimating the y2k problem. Only a year ago, estimates were running about $1 per line of code to fix the problem versus today's higher estimates. In spite of new innovative techniques such as "windowing" (the use of logic to determine the correct century, i.e., 50-99 means a century of 19 and 00-49 means a century of 20), companies continue to oversimplify the fixing of the date problem. Companies continue to understate the scope of the problem by not comprehensively including the six types of systems that have to be considered. As a result, senior management of these companies are lying back waiting for their cios to convince them that there is a real problem.

The company is especially vulnerable if its cio is weak. Red flags of a weak cio to watch for include:
- Has the cio been invisible to senior management and the board?
- Have the cio's contributions been questionable as a member of the senior management team?
- Does the cio tend to "sugar coat" tough problems?
- Has there been a pattern of late projects, and/or feature deficient projects?
- Does the cio come from a non-technical background, and show tendencies of either avoiding technical problems, or being "snowed" by technical problems?[1]

The y2k problem is hard to explain. It is even harder to explain to a recalcitrant, "show me," out-of-touch senior executive. These are

1 These "red flags" were highlighted to me during a discussion with Robert DiStefano, cio of Vanguard, about the ideas in this foreword.

dangerous situations, ones in which the board must take an aggressive role investigating and sizing the Y2K problem.

As important, once the Y2K problem is identified and sized, it must be appropriately resourced. Hard decisions have to be faced. For openers, it most likely means that new development will have to be put on hold for the next two years. Implementing such a decision will elicit a hue and cry from powerful profit center managers.

Further, the bottom line will most likely be negatively affected by a significant expense item which produces little of value except for allowing the company to stay in business beyond the year 2000. It is not surprising that many companies are simply in denial, and those that acknowledge the problem are under-budgeting for the resources they need to fix the problem.

Only high level intervention, such as at the board of director's level, is effective for turning this kind of situation around. It generally takes a few rounds for the senior management to fully internalize the financial magnitude of the Y2K problem. As a first approximation, an estimate can be made of the lines of code of the company's applications portfolio, which will generally exclude PC-based system and embedded systems. Then a range can be estimated by multiplying the lines of codes by the low and high cost per line of code for correction date problems ($2 to $6). This estimate will generally be in the tens of millions of dollars and should get attention. From the rough estimate, the real work of managing the costs and risks can proceed.

Project Management is Critical to Fixing the Problem

Having described the size and dimensions of the problem, it should be obvious that the problem cannot be resolved by brute force. Instead, the problem must be managed in such a way as to balance cost with business risk. Both project management and risk management are appropriate here.

A key step is to develop an overall project plan based upon priorities, and an individual project plan for each system that has to be worked on. It is also important to group systems and project plans by individual business units so that the senior level managers responsible are aware of their risks of system failures, and can assist in mobilizing functional resources required to fix the problem.

By periodically monitoring the project plan, real learning can be leveraged for clever ways to deal with the various kinds of problems involved in both fixing, and managing the risk of Y2K.

PRUDENT ACTIONS TO PREPARE FOR THE Y2K IMPACT

CURRENT ESTIMATES are that over fifty percent of US companies will not have fixed their Y2K problem or managed their business operational risks to acceptable levels. I think that the percentage is likely to be even higher – too many companies have been tardy in recognizing the problem and getting started on fixing it.

Whether you are in good shape or not, however, there are a number of Y2K related actions that are prudent to get underway immediately, if you have not already done so.

Don't Leave Your Public Auditors in the Dark

Public auditors are just becoming aware of the nature of the Y2K problem, and the way that it could impact the financial performance of their clients. An AICPA Year 2000 task force has recently released a report that should be reviewed by the company's Project 2000 team, and board of directors oversight committee.

In light of the auditor's "due diligence" obligation, the potentially disastrous impact on a company's operations of not being Year 2000 compliant, and possible liability suits (which are not something new to auditors), the auditor's conservative approach to the Y2K problem should be planned for, and expected.

Understanding the esoteric nature of the Y2K problem is non-trivial. While most of the big accounting firms also have IT consulting operations, there is no guarantee that these capabilities are sufficient to adequately access the risk of Year 2000 non-compliant exposure in the company's use of IT.

Nevertheless, the auditor's guiding standards for detecting errors and irregularities that reach financial statement level of materiality (SAS #53) and the more basic opinion on the auditor's consideration of an entity's ability to continue as a going concern (SAS #59) will result in every auditor getting into the Y2K problem with company management. At a minimum, expect a disclosure footnote to an "unqualified opinion" where the auditor has determined that the company has a Y2K corrective program designed and in implementation, but cannot not determine the ultimate success or failure of the program.

If such a note is not agreed to by management or no such Y2K plan exists, the auditor is likely to issue an "except for," or more precisely a "qualified" opinion. A qualified opinion is a "red flag" to the financial community, and could have an immediate impact on the company's stock price and bond rating. In fact, some loans include covenants that automatically trigger "immediately due" language if the debtor receives a "qualified" opinion from independent auditors.

It is prudent to set up a series of high level meetings with the auditor including the CEO, CFO, and CIO. If your company has a good internal auditing function, involve this group with the overall company Y2K project plan and the monitoring of the plan. The internal auditing group can also prove invaluable in working with the external auditors and keeping them up to speed on status and progress being made. The more informed the external auditing team is on the nature of the company's Y2K problem and programs to deal with it, the better for everyone.

Work With Your Legal Counsel

Legal suits have already begun. One of the first has been a supermarket chain bringing suit against a software vendor that developed its point of sale cash register system. Customers came in with new credit cards that expired after the year 2000. The cash registers did not recognize the expiration of these new cards, and rejected the customer's credit. Lines formed behind the registers, customers became angry and left, and business was lost. We will see more and more surprises like these where injury is incurred, and accountability is sought.

The estimated cost of legal suits from the consequences of not resolving the problem by the year 2000 is estimated at more than $1 trillion. Even if the real number is not this high, it is reasonable to assume an estimate in excess of the estimate of fixing the problem, which reflects a potential feeding frenzy for a lawyers' bonanza – the problem is esoteric; discovery costly and disruptive; legal fees and settlement costs will be big money.

Make your legal department part of the Y2K team. Make sure that your legal department knows very clearly that their most important performance objective is to keep the company out of court. You need lawyers informed about the nature and risks of the Y2K problem.

Already we are seeing Y2K-naive lawyers imposing tough covenants on vendors, requiring that "you, our vendor or outsourcer, will be 'Y2K compliant' or we will not continue to do business with you." Some of the vendors have just signed the contracts, not really knowing what is involved in becoming Y2K compliant; other vendors just refuse to sign, and nothing happens – the company still continues to do business with them. Many smaller vendors don't have the resources to fix the problem, and will probably just disappear after the year 2000. The false sense of security of thinking that contracts are going to alleviate this problem for the company is not only dangerous and naive, but wastes a lot of time now, and even more when blame, fault and damages are to be determined.

Alert the Board to Possible Personal Liability

If a public company fails to disclose its Y2K problem on its annual report, and experiences significant business losses, shareholder suits against the management and board of directors is a real possibility. Even if Y2K disclosure is made in the annual report and losses are incurred, shareholder suits are still possible.

In the event of Y2K suits, directors may be held personally accountable for "due diligence" in oversight of the Y2K program and corrective program executed by the company. The "business judgment rule" will come into play, which essentially protects directors from court review and liability for honest mistakes of business judgment. However, if the company did not have a Y2K corrective program, and there is little evidence of oversight monitoring of the program, the directors may find themselves in a very uncomfortable position with frightening financial liability.

While it is becoming more and more difficult, it is prudent for the board to obtain qualified third-party opinions on assessing the adequacy of a company's efforts to ensure that they will be Year 2000 compliant. Some firms will only offer what are becoming known as "negative opinions" – that is, they will alert the company if they think you are not doing something that you should be doing to be Year 2000 compliant.

Further, it is also prudent to review the company's insurance policies for business interruption and directors and officers liability to make sure that coverage includes Y2K eventualities.

Independent boards of directors are an important governance structure for corporations. Yet, the esoteric nature of the Y2K problem could result in putting board members in a tough position defending their actions (or lack thereof) in respect to the current business judgment doctrine. If this happens, companies will experience even more difficulties attracting qualified independent directors to serve on their boards.

CONCLUSIONS

YES, Y2K is a big deal. Over half of US companies are tardy, and must manage their risk of business disruption and expensive lawsuits. Aggressive action is required including involving auditors and lawyers now. Where should you start? Well, you should have started already. However, no matter what phase of problem resolution your company (and your business partners) is in, you should assess your position and risk using the guidelines in this book. With it, you have a tool to quickly assess how well you are doing to defuse your time bomb. In addition, this same approach can be used to assess your business partners and major clients.

Time is short. So is this book. Take a minute to make sure that the train you are on is going to the right destination. But don't take too long. There just isn't time!

R. L. Nolan
April 1998

Introduction

THE YEAR 2000 computer problem has the potential to affect the integrity and functioning of business operations in every company.

It is essential that every business executive be able to assess the status of his own company's Year 2000 efforts and that of those in the company's business network – partners, customers, etc. – and be able to determine if those companies will be able to maintain the integrity and normal functioning of their business operations as the year 2000 approaches and passes.

The December, Cap Gemini sponsored, 1997 Year 2000 Survey conducted by Rubin Systems (sample size 108 companies), concluded that, of those surveyed:

- 60% of companies have completed a full assessment of their inventory,
- Only 1 in 3 have detailed plans in place,
- 1 in 5 claim to have a full program in place.

As a consequence of these findings, it is clear that is it necessary to ask companies more than simply if they have a Year 2000 program in place. Having a program in place does in no way guarantee that a company is making adequate progress towards this deadline driven event.

Therefore, to assess the status of a company, it is necessary to ask high level questions that focus on the actions they should be taking and then probe one or two levels deeper to assess the soundness of those actions and calibrate the level of progress being made in executing those actions.

There are both qualitative and quantitative aspects to be evaluated in the context of assessing the potential for a customer's dealing with Year 2000 issues successfully. In this context, the QuickSTATus approach is designed to get to the core of the matter quickly while supplying you with the necessary probes to really understand what is going on.

The QuickSTATus approach allows you to get an approximation of the risk associated with a Year 2000 project. It looks at the key elements of project success:

- Having a well-defined project/program with clear accountability;
- Having a clear business view of the problem;
- Having a well defined plan that links technical and business priorities;
- Having appropriate tracking and oversight in the context of risk management;
- Having the right (and adequate) technical and business resources assigned to the project;
- Having the right testing procedures and processes in place;
- Having contingencies identified and contingency plans ready to be put into action.

The QuickSTATus assessment technique uses two levels of questions to assess a Year 2000 project. The question sets were developed to provide an approximation of Year 2000 risk based on experiences derived from surveying the status of hundreds of Year 2000 projects over the past three years and hands-on involvement in Year 2000 projects. The high level questions, and the associated certainty of your responses, provide you with a quick rating of the project's chances of success. However, if the certainty of any of the answers that you've supplied is low, there is a second drill-down question set that enables you to get the detail you need to supply a high certainty response.

The QuickSTATus assessment method involves two steps to apply it to any organization:

STEP 1:

ANSWER the QuickSTATus Test questions 1 through 10. For each question:
- Indicate your response, 0-10, with 0 being absolute no and 10 being absolute yes;
- Rate the certainty of your response from 0-100%;
- Compute the weighted rating by multiplying your response by the certainty percentage;
- Compute the total score by adding the results of each question.

Based on your results, you will have a preliminary Year 2000 assessment that should be interpreted on the scale that is presented in the next section.

STEP 2:

FOR ANY QuickSTATus questions for which the certainty is below 80%, or for those questions where you feel you need additional information to help you answer the question:

- Locate the drill down question set related to the high level question;
- Answer the five detailed questions;
- Sum up your responses, giving yourself 2 points for each yes response;
- Use this result as the response value on the main QuickSTATus response form.

INTERPRETING YOUR SCORE

To RATE your results use the following scale:[2]

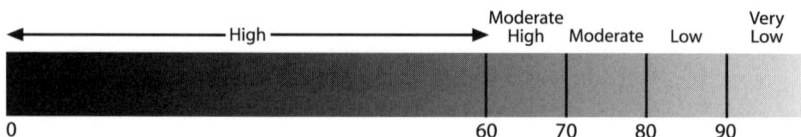

		Moderate High	Moderate	Low	Very Low
◀——————————High——————————▶					
0		60 70	80	90	

If the sum of the weighted responses is below 60, the Year 2000 project is in serious danger. If the weighted ratings fall above 80, then you are probably doing all of the right things to assure that the Year 2000 problem is being addressed for your organization. Between 60 and 80, you should be very concerned that some aspect of the effort may cause you to not succeed. If this is the case, we provide some guidance in a later section: What To Do Next.

In addition, some questions in the set are "show stoppers." If the rating of questions 1, 3, or 6 is below 30, then the project being assessed is at high risk, regardless of the total score. Again, proceed to the drill-down questions to assess what is really going on.

As we will discuss later, this technique can (and should) be applied not only to your own project but also to those of organizations in your business network.

---

2   A rule-based tool to score your results is in devlopment. For more information, contact the authors.

QuickSTATus Test

No.	Question	Rating 1-10	Cert. %	Wtd. Rating
1	Do you have a defined and funded Year 2000 project that reports into senior business management?			
2	Has the business impact of the Year 2000 problem been assessed in terms of functions, systems, liability, business partners, customers, etc.?			
3	Do you have clearly defined milestones and detailed plans in place for achieving these milestones?			
4	Do the milestones in your plan reflect your business priorities?			
5	Based on your plans, do you have adequate skilled resources in place to deal with all dimensions of the problem in the required timeframe?			
6	Are you tracking the milestones in a timely manner that allows you to take appropriate actions?			
7	Does the project have appropriate business involvement for testing, communication, business exposure, and regulatory compliance?			
8	Does accountability for the success of your Year 2000 project lie directly with business management?			
9	Are you planning to test all business operations to assure that they will operate properly for pre- and post-Year 2000 processing?			
10	Have you created alternatives for all critical business operations in case they do not function properly for pre- and post-Year 2000 processing?			
	Total:			

Ratings: 0 = No 10 = Absolute Yes Certainty = 0-100%

DRILL-DOWN QUESTIONS

1. Do you have a defined and funded Year 2000 project that reports into senior business management?

The Year 2000 must be viewed as a business problem, and not a technical problem. The size and scope of this effort is greater than any that most companies have dealt with. It requires the involvement of all parts of the company, and must be positioned as the number one business priority. It requires dedicated funding and complete business management commitment. It will require quick decisions and the direct involvement of the board. It can not be accomplished in a random, haphazard basis by lower level IT management.

Drill-Down Questions:

No.	Question	Y/N
1.1	Is there a specific budget for your Year 2000 project that includes all anticipated costs?	
1.2	Are you tracking actual expenses versus estimates?	
1.3	Is there a dedicated program office and appropriate project offices to manage the Year 2000 project?	
1.4	Does the overall Year 2000 program report to the CEO, COO, or President?	
1.5	Does an inventory of all affected components exist (applications, hardware, facilities, etc.)?	
	Award 2 points for each YES answer.	
	Score:	

2. Has the business impact of the Year 2000 problem been assessed in terms of functions, systems, liability, business partners, customers, etc.?

The Year 2000 is much more than a systems problem, which has gotten most of the publicity. The ramifications of a failure to complete all aspects of the work are potentially catastrophic. A multi-view approach is needed and all areas of "Doomsday" concern must be addressed, both within an organization, and externally through all of the supply and distribution channels. No one is alone, and all interdependencies must be understood and addressed.

Drill-Down Questions:

No.	Question	Y/N
2.1	Are the effects of Year 2000 on earnings, liquidity, capital, and mergers and acquisitions understood?	
2.2	Is there representation from all core business functions (legal, procurement, audit, facilities, etc.)?	
2.3	Have all business networks been mapped, with identification of all interfaces & interdependencies?	
2.4	Have you contacted all third parties and received written certification of Year 2000 readiness?	
2.5	Are you in close contact and coordination with industry groups and customers?	
	Award 2 points for each YES answer.	
	Score:	

3. Do you have clearly defined milestones and detailed plans in place for achieving these milestones?

The Year 2000 is not a problem that will fix itself. There is no magic cure, and it requires the hard work of many dedicated resources. Every moment is precious and must be well planned out. Each task must be understood and the right resources applied. All interdependencies need to be understood, and interim milestones established to allow you a level of confidence that progress – the right progress – is being made. Remember, it is what you don't know and haven't planned for that will kill you.

Drill-Down Questions:

No.	Question	Y/N
3.1	Have all plans been created utilizing consistent project steps and estimating guidelines?	
3.2	Does a single view of system and non-system Year 2000 activities exist as one plan?	
3.3	Do adequate buffers exist within all plans for unforeseen activities and delays?	
3.4	Are the plans at a sufficient level of granularity to assure identification of necessary resources?	
3.5	Do plans exist for associated activities, such as system retirements, new system implementation?	
	Award 2 points for each YES answer.	
	Score:	

4. Do the milestones in your plan reflect your business priorities?

Most businesses will not be able to do everything, creating the need for business triage. The single greatest factor in preventing a company from completing all Year 2000 activities will be the lack of synchronization with business priorities. In other words, business as usual will take priority over the Year 2000. A little extra enhancement will "be okay." It is not! Unless mechanisms are in place to continually review priorities and ensure an organization-wide view of what must be done, the probability of triage will increase.

Drill-Down Questions:

No.	Question	Y/N
4.1	Is there direct business input into Year 2000 plans and plan reviews?	
4.2	Do Year 2000 plans and priorities mesh with business plans?	
4.3	Is there a clear mechanism to revise plans based on changes in business priorities?	
4.4	Is there a regular management review of business and Year 2000 priorities?	
4.5	Does a clear escalation process exist to resolve prioritization issues?	
	Award 2 points for each YES answer.	
	Score:	

5. Based on your plans, do you have adequate skilled resources in place to deal with all dimensions of the problem in the required timeframe?

The Year 2000 is one problem that money alone can't solve. It requires the application of skilled and knowledgeable resources that are familiar with your business and technical environments. In addition, technical resources in the marketplace are scarce, and for the most part have already been secured by the top-tier companies. As for skilled business resources, it is hard to deploy business people on a seemingly non-value added project. Therefore, deployment of resources must be rapid and well-planned.

Drill-Down Questions:

No.	Question	Y/N
5.1	Do you have detailed resource plans in place for both people and technical capacity?	
5.2	Do you have staff retention plans for all critical resources?	
5.3	Do you have an adequate number people resources specifically identified for the Year 2000 project?	
5.4	Do you have adequate technology resources available for testing and contingency?	
5.5	Do you have procurement plans in place for acquiring needed additional resources?	
	Award 2 points for each YES answer.	
	Score:	

6. Are you tracking the milestones in a timely manner that allows you to take appropriate actions?

The law of inertia states that without force a body will remain at rest. For application maintenance areas, this means that without constant vigilance and frequent milestone reporting of progress, the Year 2000 project will stall out. A standard and consistent set of success measures are required, and must be presented to business management on a regular basis. In addition, the criticality of the problem demands quick decision making and proactive management. There is little time for discussion and consensus building.

Drill-Down Questions:

No.	Question	Y/N
6.1	Do status reports go to senior business management?	
6.2	Are you tracking milestones planned for completion versus actual?	
6.3	Are you tracking risks and issues separately?	
6.4	Do you have escalation procedures for high-risk projects and issue resolution?	
6.5	Are you tracking operational progress (the ability of a business function to operate in the Year 2000)?	
	Award 2 points for each YES answer.	
	Score:	

7. Does the project have appropriate business involvement for testing, communication, business exposure, and regulatory compliance?

As previously stated, the Year 2000 is a business problem. Therefore, it will require the involvement of a large number of dedicated business managers. Business knowledge is key, and this comes into play particularly in the area of testing. Equipment will be available, but only so much work can be funneled through a limited number of business analysts. In addition, it is the business areas that must communicate with customers, and understand and plan for risks. This is not an area that can be underestimated or assumed to be available.

Drill-Down Questions:

No.	Question	Y/N
7.1	Have dedicated/specific business resources been allocated to all required Year 2000 activities?	
7.2	Are there appropriate levels of business participation in test planning?	
7.3	Is business represented at key external meetings with industry groups and customers/suppliers?	
7.4	Are business and legal involved in plan, review, and execution of external communication?	
7.5	Is a continuous analysis performed on all business risks and exposure areas?	
	Award 2 points for each YES answer.	
	Score:	

8. Does accountability for the success of your Year 2000 project lie directly with business management?

The Year 2000 effort must be coordinated centrally to ensure all activities are accomplished in a fashion that addresses the many demands of the project (e.g., legal implications, coordinated communications, board involvement, etc.). However, this does not mean that accountability can be delegated upwards. The Year 2000 is a competitive and survival issue, and ultimate accountability must reside directly with line business managers.

Drill-Down Questions:

No.	Question	Y/N
8.1	Are Year 2000 goals and milestone achievements tied to management business objectives (MBOs)?	
8.2	Is there formal business signoff certifying the readiness of your organization?	
8.3	Is Year 2000 funding reflected as a separate line item in business area budgets?	
8.4	Will compensation be impacted (positively and negatively) based on Year 2000 results?	
8.5	Do all projects report status directly to line business executives?	
	Award 2 points for each YES answer.	
	Score:	

9. Are you planning to test all business operations to assure that they will operate properly for pre- and post-Year 2000 processing?

The success of the Year 2000 effort will ultimately come down to how well you test. At least 50% of the overall time and cost of Year 2000 work will be related to testing, and its scope requires extensive, detailed planning and coordination. Through testing, a necessary comfort level can be provided to allow for signoff on completion of efforts. In addition, you will be able to state with confidence that Year 2000 problems have been resolved for your organization – without fear of later allegations of misrepresentation.

Drill-Down Questions:

No.	Question	Y/N
9.1	Do you understand when the Year 2000 will affect each business function?	
9.2	Have test environments been sized and established for Year 2000 testing?	
9.3	Has an adequate level of capacity been allowed for internal and external partner testing?	
9.4	Does a common certification definition exist, and are business signoffs required at each level?	
9.5	Do formal quality assurance and change control processes exist?	
	Award 2 points for each YES answer. **Score:**	

10. Have you created alternatives for all your critical business operations in case they do not function properly for pre- and post-Year 2000 processing?

The Year 2000 problem is affecting everyone at roughly the same time. You can not expect everyone to succeed at 100% levels. There is no way to know at what point in the business partner network problems might/will occur. Therefore, you must understand the most likely points of failure and prepare your organization and customers for likely impacts.

Drill-Down Questions:

No.	Question	Y/N
10.1	Has scenario analysis been performed, identifying critical failure points within your business network?	
10.2	Have you reviewed the Year 2000 readiness of your supply chain and distribution channels?	
10.3	Have you had face-to-face meetings with major business partners?	
10.4	Have your business networks been scored and alternatives planned for high probability failures?	
10.5	Have you reviewed environmental infrastructures (e.g., utilities, phones, mass transit, etc.)?	
	Award 2 points for each YES answer.	
	Score:	

Robbins-Rubin Year 2000
Performance Indices

In order to truly understand the progress of an organization's Year 2000 efforts, the following two questions need to be answered in a concise and simple way.

Is the project proceeding at the planned pace in terms of work being performed to bring the organization toward implementing a Year 2000 business environment?

Is the Year 2000 business environment becoming operational within the required timeframe?

A series of indicators are presented in this section that effectively track and report Year 2000 project progress and Year 2000 solution implementation separately. Both sets of indicators provides concise management information in a three-dimensional view:

- Progress in terms of Year 2000 impacted entities being worked on in the Year 2000 conversion process ("Work in Progress");
- Progress in terms of milestone completion in Year 2000 conversion process plans;
- Overall progress in terms of Year 2000 project schedule performance: ahead, behind, or on target from a process viewpoint.

Paralleling the view of progress, a set of implementation measures are also presented. These focus on:

- Progress in terms of entities being put into operation;
- Progress in terms of milestone completion in Year 2000 implementation plans;
- Overall progress in terms of Year 2000 operational implementation performance: ahead, behind, or on target from a operational viewpoint.

Combined, we have termed these the Robbins-Rubin Year 2000 Performance Indices, or RRI. With these, a company will be able to gauge both its internal performance in making progress toward implementing its Year 2000 solution set and be able to communicate its progress in a concise, clear, and meaningful manner.

The primary progress metrics appearing in media analyses of Year 2000 progress is "percent of systems compliant." This metric can be misleading for a variety of reasons:

- Definitions of compliance vary;
- Most organizational strategies involve testing before compliance is declared, hence the buildup of this metric will be low until 1999 for most enterprises;
- There are more aspects to the Year 2000 problem than just "systems."

It is therefore proposed that a new approach be used for both high level internal and external progress reporting at a company. It is based upon the following:

- Progress toward Year 2000 success consists, in part, of having systems and non-systems "work in progress." That is to say that system or non-system entities for which a Year 2000 impact have been identified are either being assessed, converted, replaced, or tested.
- Progress towards Year 2000 success consists, in part, of making progress through major milestones in a Year 2000 plan.
- Progress towards Year 2000 success is finally determined by having system or non-system entities that either have been remediated or replaced put into operation successfully.

Given the above, it is proposed that Year 2000 progress be measured from a "work in progress" perspective *and* an implementation/operation perspective.

THE YEAR 2000 "WORK IN PROGRESS" PERSPECTIVE METRICS

THREE METRICS are proposed to give a complete view of Work in Progress (WIP). All can be applied to system and non-system entities.

Percent of entities for which work is in progress:

This metric is an indicator of the percentage of entities for which assessment, conversion, replacement, testing or other remediation work is taking place. Its computation requires a count of total entities impacted by Year 2000 and a method to be able to track the total number that are at any stage of the Year 2000 process cycle. This is essentially an entity penetration metric: how much of what you know about is actually in progress.

Percent of milestones completed:

Using the master project plan as a base, this metric is an indicator of the percent of milestones have been logged as completed. This is a timeline/event based progress indicator.

Robbins-Rubin Index-Schedule (RRI-S)

This is the indicator as to whether or not the Year 2000 will complete successfully on time.
RRI-S is computed as follows:

$$\frac{\text{Total number of entities for which work is in progress} \times \text{Current milestones completed}}{\text{Total number of entities for which work should be in progress} \times \text{Planned milestones to have been completed}}$$

The resulting index is interpreted as follows:
- If this ratio is greater than 1, work is ahead of schedule both in completing schedules milestone and processing entities.
- If it is equal to 1, then all is proceeding as planned.
- If it is less than 1, then either the schedule or milestone completion rate is slipping.

Year 2000 schedule acceleration can be computed by $1 -$ RRI-S. This shows the amount of speed up (as a percent of schedule when multiplied by 100) for a Year 2000 project to get back on schedule.

Getting A Complete Progress Picture

The Year 2000 project involves:
- Systems;
- Infrastructure/Technical Environment;
- Distribution Computing Networks and Desktop Applications;
- Non-System Entities.

It is suggested that these three metrics used to calculate RRI-S be computed for each of these areas separately. They can then be weighted (to a total of 100%) by the importance of each of these four areas to compute a RRI-S for the entire Year 2000 program.

The metrics can also be computed by each project, project office, or business unit depending on how the underlying data is structured.

THE YEAR 2000 OPERATIONAL PERSPECTIVE

USING THE SAME metrics techniques, the buildup of Year 2000 operational capability can be assessed as follows:

Percent of entities which are Year 2000 operational:
This metric is an indicator of the percentage of entities which have completed the entire Year 2000 process, have been validated for proper post-Year 2000 performance, and are in operation. Computation requires a count of total entities impacted by Year 2000 and a method to be able to track the total number that meet the operational criteria described.

Percent of milestones completed:
Using the part of the master project plan that involves the movement of Year 2000 processed entities into operation as a base, this metric is an indicator of what percent of milestones in this process subset have been logged as completed.

Robbins-Rubin Index – Operational (RRI-O):
This is the indicator of Year 2000 completion.
RRI-O is computed as follows:

Total number of entities which are in operation
× Current operational milestones completed

Total number of entities which should be in operation
× Planned operational milestones to have been completed

If this ratio is greater than 1, operational implementation is ahead of schedule. If it is equal to 1, then all is proceeding as planned. If it is less than one, then either the schedule or operational completion rate is slipping.

Year 2000 operational schedule acceleration can be computed by 1 − RRI-O. This would show the amount of speed up (as a percent of schedule when multiplied by 100) for a Year 2000 project to get on operational schedule.

Getting the Complete Year 2000 Performance Picture

Using both the progress metrics set and the operational metrics set (RRI-S and RRI-O) will provide a complete picture of the Year 2000 program. In addition, you should compute a weighted metric (weighting more toward operational) by combining the progress and operational measures to provide an overall summary.

BUSINESS NETWORK ANALYSIS

THERE ARE no standalone companies in the world today. Every organization is tied to a set of others for everything from utilities to finance to news and information. Your complete business network is likely to include all or some of the following:

- Utilities: electricity, oil, steam, gas, water;
- Banking/finance: investments, bank accounts, check processing, credit;
- Social services: police, fire, taxation, public welfare;
- Health: hospitals, doctors, medicines;
- News/media: newspapers, magazine, radio, television, films;
- Transportation: planes, trains, cars, ships, bus, bridges, tunnels;
- Education: schools, courseware, degrees, certifications;
- Communications: phone, fax, mail, Internet;
- Food: agriculture, farming, shipping;
- Government: local to federal;
- Defense: armed forces worldwide;
- Embedded systems: from toasters to elevators to cars to more;
- Computers and software companies.

In addition, your business is part of a business transaction network. Can your organization map the flows of all its transactions from people through companies through systems?

All of these – the network and the transaction flows – have Year 2000 issues. All of these should have Year 2000 projects associated with them. But the big issue is that even if your organization is dealing with the Year 2000 problem effectively, your network and transaction partners may not be at your level of year 2000 readiness. Suppose they all are doing well and your organization is not. Do you know your liability if your company "brings them down?"

Therefore, because of all of these concerns, it is critical that you assess the status of your total network. The steps to take are:

- Map out your major business networks, i.e., transaction and inter-party relationships such as utilities, government, etc.;
- Use QuickSTATus to assess their levels of risk via
  questionnaire, phone interview, or from public
  disclosure information;
- Calculate the "network reliability" with each party
  and through each transaction chain. (To do this,
  look for the highest risk rating in the chain. This
  is the weakest link and should be used to set the
  overall risk level for the entire chain);
- Identify parties of high risk and high impact and
  develop strategies to minimize or mitigate risk;
- Do the above steps quarterly until June of 1999,
  then consider doing it monthly.

Step 4 on this list – identifying parties of high risk – is particularly tricky in terms of the strategies you may have to enact. They can
take the form of anything from contingencies to bail-out.

Bail-out can be used if you are ahead and have adequate
resources to help the weaker organization with its Year 2000 project.
However, if they appear doomed to failure you need to develop a more
timely contingency. These may range from linking up with another
organization that performs a similar function, to absorbing the
work/process/function on your own, to acquiring another firm to deal
with it, to discontinuing the business activity itself. The option to be
exercised is clearly a function of the risk and value involved.

However, no matter what options you select, the issue is to focus
on the network and not just your own organization. Other sources of
support in doing this are industry associations. Many ranging from
the Information Technology Association of America to specific groups
in the banking and telecommunications industry are focusing on
issues that specifically relate to the business networks. These groups
are also attempting to propagate testing practices, compliance standards, and coordinate cross-company articulation.

In the 1992 election, the slogan "It's the economy, stupid" was the
watchword for the populace. For Year 2000 the equivalent may be "It's
the business network, stupid."

What to Do Next

USING THIS guide you should have answered the question set (or sets) for both your own enterprise and those in your business network. (It might be of significant interest for you to also check out your personal network too along with the government.)

In the context of your own organization:

- If you do not have a defined and funded project with business management accountability and oversight, bring this to your Board. It may be too late to get going internally so business contingency planning is now a must.
- If you have not assessed the business impact of the problem – all dimensions – time is of the essence. Probably the use of external consultants is the only answer while you deploy internal resources inside the organization as time ticks away.
- If you do not have a clear set of detailed milestones, you are really at risk. Hold an offsite intensive planning session; use a consultant as a facilitator; build week by week mini-plans; and get your contingency plans ready.
- If your plans, or lack of them, do not reflect business priorities, perform triage NOW!
- If you don't have the resources to pull this off, consider the position of others in your field as business process outsourcing partners; consider what consultants can do for you.
- If you don't have tracking, get a project/program management specialist into your organization right away. Create weekly "flash" reports. But don't concentrate on the successes, concentrate on what is missed and how to escalate these issues to action.
- If the business units and resources are not on board – escalate this to your board. Make the case

that this is a business problem and not a technical one.

- If you do not have business accountability established, bring this to the CEO or CFO (assuming that you are neither). Move this project's visibility to the highest level in the company.
- If you are not planning to test everything, make sure your test plans test what is core to the business and the most critical. But in the background have active contingency plans.

For certain, plan to have back-ups for all that you do in your company that may be impacted by the Year 2000. Build a risk analysis table. Consider each industry, consider each government service, and then list the risks, threats, and action you must take.[3]

There definitely is a lot to do next. Most definitely, there is not a lot of time to do it!

---

3   Another source of information is our *Year 2000 Planning Guide.* See the last page of this book for ordering information.

Resources

THIS SECTION includes a list of Year 2000 websites and contact information for other independent research organizations which have been addressing aspects of the Year 2000 problem.

Year 2000 Websites

THE FOLLOWING lists a number of Year 2000 websites that can be referenced to gain more information about the year 2000. They are increasing each day, and many maintain links to other sites.
www.
aba.com
abanet.org
auditserv.com
bai.org
bsi.org.uk/cgi-bin/fx
cinderella.co.za
cio.com/forums/year2K.html
comlinks.com/gov/omb2697.htm
compinfo.co.uk/y2k/manupos.htmwww.compinfo.co.uk/y2k/
    index.htm
computerweekly.co.uk
computerworld.com
datamation.com
dciexpo.com/2000ad
ffiec.gov/y2k
ft.com
gm-2000.com or .co.uk
infomgmtforum.com
informationweek.com
it2000.com
itaa.org
itpolicy.gsa.gov/mks/year2000/y201toc1.htm
jks.co.uk/y2ki
killen.com
mbs-program.com/project2000

microsoft.com/projects/fs_prj.htm
milberg.com
mitre.org:80/research/y2k/docs/VENDORS.html
pirkle-websites.com
s390.ibm.com:80/stories/tran2000.html
sam.pentagon.mil/yr2000/year2000.htm
sbhs.com
simnet.orgwww.simnet.org/public/mktplace/wktgrps.html
software.ibm.com/news/2bda.htm
spr.com
tamu.edu/cis/teams/yr2k/tips.application.testing.html
y2k.com
y2kinvestor.com
year2000.co.uk
year2000.com
yourdon.com
y2k.raleigh.ibm.com

In addition, we have included the websites for each research organization listed below.

INDEPENDENT RESEARCH ORGANIZATIONS

Data Process Management Association (DPMA)

The DPMA is a well-known nonprofit association of software managers and professional personnel. Like most software-oriented non-profits, the DPMA has been aware of and moving toward sharing information on the Year 2000 problem. In the case of the DPMA, they sponsor regional and national Year 2000 conferences and also are publishing a book of collected Year 2000 articles.

DPMA
Phone: 310-534-3922   Fax: 310-534-0743
Email: ttchq@ttcus.com
Web: http://www.ttcp.us.com

Digital Consulting, Inc.

DCI is a well known software conference and seminar company founded by George Schussel. DCI is a for-profit organization. DCI is primarily a conference group, with a smattering of management consulting as well. DCI sponsors a number of large conferences on the year 2000 issue in the United States and abroad.
  Digital Consulting, Inc.
  204 Andover Street
  Andover, MA 01810
  Phone: 508-470-3880   Fax: 508-470-0526
  Web: http://www.DCI.Expo.COM

Gartner Group

The Gartner Group is a for-profit research corporation that collects data on a wide variety of topics. The Gartner Group has produced a report on the global impact of the Year 2000 problem: Hall, B. and Schick, K. "Year 2000 Crisis – Estimating the Cost;" Gartner Group Application Development and Management Strategies (ADM) Research Note, Key Issue Analysis, KA-210-1262.
  Gartner Group
  Gartner Park
  Top Gallant Road
  Stamford, CT 06904
  Phone: 203-964-0096   Fax: 203-324-7901
  Web: http://gartner.com
  Email: info@gartner.com

IBC USA Conferences, Inc.

IBC is a commercial conference organizer that hosts a number of software related events. Like most conference houses, IBC has started running a series of regional Year 2000 events. Unlike some Year 2000 conferences, IBC tends toward vertical themes for specific industries such as insurance, banking, and financial services.
  IBC USA Conferences, Inc.
  225 Turnpike Road

Southborough, MA 01772-1749
Phone: 508-481-6400   Fax: 508-481-7911
Email: inq@ibcusa.com
Web: http://www.io.org/-ibc/vendor2000

The Information Technology Association of America (ITAA)

The ITAA is a non-profit association of software vendors. The ITAA has formed a Year 2000 task force under the chairmanship of Peter Sheridan of Viasoft. The ITAA has published a useful although incomplete catalog of Year 2000 vendors. Heidi Hooper at 703-284-5312 or hhooper@itaa.org are the contacts cited in the ITAA Year 2000 vendor catalog.

ITAA
1616 N. Fort Myer Drive, Suite 1300
Arlington, VA 22209
Phone: 703-522-5055   Fax: 703-525-2279
Web: http://www.itaa.org

Peter de Jager

Peter de Jager is an independent Canadian consultant, speaker, and collector of data on the Year 2000 problem. Peter runs a very popular Year 2000 web site, and is a frequent contributor of articles and lectures on the Year 2000 problem.
Peter de Jager
22 Marchbank Crescent
Brampton, Ontario L6S 3B1 Canada
Phone: 905-792-8706   Fax: 905-792-9818
Email: pdjager@hookup.net
Web: http://www.year2000.com

Robert Kendall

Robert Kendall is now an independent consultant, after retiring from the IBM corporation. While at IBM, Kendall performed a large-scale analysis of the mainframe software in eight IBM data centers. This study found, surprisingly, that dormant or inactive programs that had not been run in more than a year comprised more than half of the entire software portfolio. Assuming other corporations have a similar ratio of dormant to active applications, this study may be relevant to the Year 2000 problem by allowing enterprises to delay or avoid spending money to update dormant applications. However, it proved to be very difficult to separate the active portions from the dormant portions of software portfolios.

    Phone: 914-226-2419
    Email: Bobkend@AOL.com

Ken Orr Institute

    Ken Orr, the founder and chairman of the Ken Orr institute, is a well-known author and lecturer on a variety of software topics. He has been a frequent key note speaker at Year 2000 conferences, and has also performed a number of consulting studies in the Year 2000 domain. Ken also explores issues in the data warehouse domain. His conclusion is that U.S. companies may not be moving fast enough to solve the Year 2000 problem before the end of the century.

    Ken Orr Institute
    534 South Kansas
    Topeka, KS 66603
    Phone: 913-357-0003   Fax: 913-357-8446
    Web: http://www.kenorrinst.com

MITRE Corporation

    The MITRE Corporation is a non-profit government-sponsored research institute that deals with a large number of military technology questions. The U.S. Department of Defense sponsored a study of the military and defense implications of the Year 2000 problem. The MITRE study of the Year 2000 issue is specialized, but very thorough. The research was headed up by Thomas Backman of MITRE's Bedford laboratory. The MITRE Year 2000 research is somewhat alarming because it deals with the impact of the problem on satellites, military aircraft, military logistics, ships, weapons systems, and a number of other areas where failures can range from serious to catastrophic.

MITRE
202 Burlington Road
Bedford, MA 01730-1420
Phone: 617-271-2725   Fax: 617-271-6239
Email: tkb@mitre.org
Web: http://mitre.com

National Software Council (NSC)

The National Software Council is a fairly new non-profit organization created to assist the United States software industry in maintaining a favorable balance of trade. The NSC is still feeling its way in terms of missions, but the Year 2000 problem is obviously one that falls within the NSC purview. The current NSC president is Larry Bernstein, formerly of AT&T.
National Software Council
PO Box 4500
Alexandria, VA 22303
Phone: 703-742-7111   Fax: 703-742-7200
Email: lbernstein@worldnet.att.net

Vito Peraino

Vito Peraino is a practicing attorney in Los Angeles. He is a frequent author on the legal aspects of the Year 2000 problem, and has also appeared on radio talk shows. Because the legal implications of the Year 2000 problem are massive, it is very useful to include attorneys as part of all major Year 2000 upgrade plans.
Hancock, Rothert & Bunshoft Llp, Attorneys
515 S. Figueroa Street, 17th floor
Los Angeles, CA 90071
Phone: 213-623-7777   Fax: 213-623-5405

Rubin Systems, Inc.

Howard Rubin is a well known software lecturer, author, and researcher on a wide variety of topics. He is also the designer of the ESTIMACS software cost estimating tool, and a tenured professor of software engineering at Hunter College. Howard is a frequent keynote speaker at Year 2000 conferences and has accumulated a solid body of data on the Year 2000 issue.

Dr. Howard Rubin
PO Box 387
Pound Ridge, NY 10576
Phone: 914-764-4931   Fax: 914-764-0536
Email: howard-rubin@compuserve.com
Web: www.hrubin.com

Society of Information Management (SIM)

The Society of Information Management is a non-profit association aimed at the software management community. SIM has a Year 2000 working group that is accumulating data and information on the Year 2000 problem. The co-chairman is Dr. Leon Kappelman of the University of North Texas.

Leon A. Kappelman
Business Computer Information Systems
Associate Director, College of Business Administration
University of North Texas
PO Box 13677
Denton, TX 76203
Phone: 817-565-3110   Fax: 817-565-4935
Email: kapp@unt.edu

Software Testing Assurance Corporation

The Software Testing Assurance Corporation provides independent certification of Y2000 readiness through the application of public certification standards. Such certification becomes a condition for obtaining Y2000 insurance policies. The Software Testing Assurance Corporation was founded by Paul A. Strassmann, now Chairman and CEO. Prominent members of management include DuWayne Peterson.

Paul A. Strassmann
Software Testing Assurance Corporation
Six Landmark Square

Stamford, CT 06901
Phone: 203-966-5505   Fax: 203-966-5506
Email: CEO@STACorp.com

Ernest Auerbach
Software Testing Assurance Corporation
300 Park Avenue
New York, NY 10022
Phone: 212-572-6319   Fax: 212-572-6488
Email: COO@STACorp.com

Software Management Network

Software Management Network is a publishing, consulting, and teaching group that specializes in techniques and technology to manage installed software systems. It was founded by Nicholas Zvegintzov, whose unusual specialty is methods and problems of maintaining existing software. Software Management Network maintains information on technology for handling the Year 2000 problem, and trains groups on how to manage, carry out, and test Year 2000 conversion.

Software Management Network
B10 – Suite 237
4546 El Camino Real
Los Altos CA 94022 USA
Phone: 650-941-4027   Fax: 650-941-4028
Emai:l smn_jmg@compuserve.com
Web: http://www.softwaremanagement.com

Software Productivity Group (SPG)

SPG is a for-profit conference, seminar, research, and publication company. Among their various offerings is the well-known software journal *Application Development Trends* edited by John Desmond. SPG also sponsors are variety of conferences and seminars on Year 2000 issues. SPG and the next company in this listing, Software Productivity Research (SPR), have similar names, but have no direct business relationship. This same statement is also true for the Software

Productivity Consortium (spc), Software Engineering Institute (sei), and Software Research Associates (sra).
Software Productivity Group, Inc.
386 West Main Street, Suite 2
Northboro, MA 01532
Phone: 508-393-7100   Fax: 508-393-3388

Software Productivity Research, Inc. (spr)

Software Productivity Research, Inc. (spr) is a for-profit research, development, and management consulting company located in Burlington, Massachusetts. spr was formed in 1984. Capers Jones is the spr Chairman. spr has been actively collecting data on the economic impact of the Year 2000 problem, as can be seen from the report itself.
Software Productivity Research, Inc.
1 New England Executive Park
Burlington, MA 01803-5005
Phone: 617-273-0140   Fax: 617-273-5176
Web: http://www.spr.com
Email: Capers@spr.com

SPR

This company and the previous company, Software Productivity Research, share the spr initials but do not have any direct business connection. This second spr was formed in 1973 and is a mid-western corporation specializing in maintenance, renovation, and Year 2000 software updates. The president is Rob Figliulo. Both of the sprs collect data on the Year 2000 issue, and both are occasionally mistaken for the other. Fortunately there is no direct competition between the two sprs.
spr
2105 Spring Road, 7th floor
Oak Brook, IL 60521
Phone: 708-990-2040   Fax: 708-990-2062
Web: www.sprinc.com

Software Technology Support Center (STSC)

The Software Technology Support Center is a non-profit organization funded by the US Air Force and located at Hill Air Force Base in Ogden, Utah. STSC performs research in a variety of software-related topics including the Year 2000 problem. STSC is also the publisher of the military software journal, *Crosstalk*, which is surprisingly lively and interesting for a government journal. One of the STSC Year 2000 researchers, Bryce Ragland, has written a useful book that is being published by McGraw-Hill: *The Year 2000 Problem Solver: A Five-Step Disaster Prevention Plan.*

Software Technology Support Center
ALC/TISE
7278 Fourth Street
Hill AFB, UT 84056-5205
Phone: 801-777-8068   Fax: 801-777-8069
Web: http://www.stsc.hill.af.mil
Email: stscols@software.hill.af.mil

WSR Consulting Group

The WSR consulting group occupies an interesting niche: management, technology, and litigation consulting. The founder and president, Warren Reid, is not an attorney but rather a management consultant who specializes in intellectual property and software litigation. Warren frequently works as an expert witness in arbitration and litigation involving software issues. Obviously, the Year 2000 problem will be a fruitful domain for litigation. Warren is a frequent writer and speaker at Year 2000 events, and tends to stress the legal issues, which other speakers and authors may not be aware of.

WSR Consulting Group
4273 Noeline Avenue, Suite 200
Encino, CA 91436
Phone: 818 986 8842   Fax: 818 986 7955
Email: consult@primenet.com

Afterword

The Direct and Indirect Economic Consequences of the Year 2000 Computer Crisis

Dr. Howard A. Rubin

MY FRIEND and colleague, Capers Jones, recently prepared an impact analysis of possible Year 2000 scenarios and their economic consequences to highlight the importance of this problem:

Y2K Problems Repaired (%)	Y2K Problems Not Repaired (%)	Economic and Political Impact of Unrepaired Year 2000 Problems
100	0	None
95	5	Local for some enterprises
90	10	Significant for many enterprises
85	15	Severe: best case for United States
80	20	Severe: possible recession
75	25	Severe: best case for European Union
70	30	Very severe: possible depression
65	35	Very severe: depression probable
60	40	Very severe: political crises
55	45	Very severe: martial law probable
50	50	Very severe: governments fail
45	55	Very severe: bankruptcies common
40	60	Very severe: unemployment >35%
35	65	Crisis level: infrastructure crippled
30	70	Crisis level: infrastructure collapses
25	75	Crisis level: famines probable

Source: Capers Jones, Software Productivity Research, Burlington, MA

It is clear that the Year 2000 computer crisis has both direct and indirect economic consequences for business. The direct consequences have to do with the ability of businesses to conduct business itself as the millennium approaches and is eventually upon us. The indirect consequences are what might be considered to be "second order" effects – these have to do with the impact on the business of the diversion of resources to work on the Year 2000 computer crisis.

It is evident new factors are driving economic and business success in today's information and knowledge based economy. If you follow the media, the following sound bites are pretty common:

> "Ideas and technological discoveries are the driving engines of economic growth."
> Source: *The Wall Street Journal*, 1/21/97

> "In the future, the ability to learn faster than your competitors may be the only sustainable competitive advantage."
> Source: Peter Senge, *The Fifth Discipline*

> "In order to remain competitive, today's corporation must develop and understanding of global technology economics. Software development work now can flow freely to whomever can deliver the most effective and efficient product regardless of time zone or national border. Adam Smith would be proud!"
> Source: CIO *Magazine*, 2/1/97

> "The problem with the future is that it's not what it used to be!"
> Source: Michael Hammer, 10/89

Jim Manzi, formerly CEO of Lotus, once cited a figure in an interview on one of my videotapes that technology spending in the 1980s – the entire decade – totaled $800 billion dollars. It looks like the worldwide figure for this decade, the 1990s will be in the $3 trillion to $4 trillion dollar range. The implications of these figures are astounding! Quite simply, in every two-year period in the 1990s, we are virtually reliving the entire spending of the 1980s. And this statement is simply based on the average spending. The averages do not tell the whole story because technology options and opportunities are constantly expanding. This in turn implies that the rate of spending is most likely constantly accelerating. If you look at trends in IT spending in a few key industry groups, you'll see a major upwards change, averaging an almost 37% increase in IT budget between 1995 and 1996, in the top performing companies.

The bottom line, the first of a few that I will mention here, is that we are living a 5 to 1 compression or fast-forward phenomena over the previous decade. Therefore, it is imperative that trends in the dispersion of information technology and information itself must be considered in formulating business strategy today. What are these trends? I see five basic ones:

- Computing power is becoming a household commodity;
- Connectivity and the ability to move information around the world in an instant is increasing geometrically;
- The capability to build effective software is the key to leveraging raw computing power;
- Connectivity and the change in the distribution of computing power are being harnessed most effectively by businesses that can align them with their business strategies;
- Technology "agility" – being able to align technology use with business opportunity on demand – is an essential element of business success.

These in turn imply that the capabilities to create, maintain, and use software and information/knowledge systems are critical business competencies and are becoming national core competencies. However, competitive advantage and success require that these capabilities be used wisely. The investments made must produce business value in order to be meaningful.

The top 500 companies in the US today spend about $100B within their information technology organizations, employ more than 500,000 professionals in this area, and spend in excess of $6,000 per employee on information technology per year. (By the way, these are the dollars under the control of the IT organization. A rough guesstimate is that true spending is approximately twice this figure.)

The big question that any executive should ask is "What am I (we) getting for that the $6,000 investment (expense, from some points of view)?" The average company supports $48 in revenue per employee per IT dollar and $1.15 in income per employee per IT dollar. The most effective support $895 in revenue per employee and $47 in income per employee – a 19:1 and 41:1 higher yield per dollar.

Please notice that I chose to use the word "support" in these statements. In no way do I want to imply that spending more per employee produces business results on its own. Those companies that are the most effective literally make it happen. Best in class at IT yield management have a few basic practices in place. These are cost management and benefits management. The former focuses on establishing a chart of accounts and understanding IT from an almost activity based costing view. They know where their money is being spent and can allocate it across processes and people. The latter focuses on getting the yield from their investments. They not only generate business cases for their projects and work. They actively manage to get those benefits.

The cost management side is illustrated by the latest data relating to what IT organizations and businesses know about their systems assets. In 1991, I published my first, somewhat notorious, information systems "black hole" findings. The basic results were:

- Only 1 in 5 companies had information of the size of their applications portfolio;
- Only 1 in 30 companies had information of how the size of their applications portfolio changed from year to year (I call this portfolio flux and the magic number, somewhat pi-like, is 15%);
- Only 1 in 100 companies had information of the quality of their information systems.

My data for the first half of 1997 is now being crunched and the preliminary analysis are not quite ready for prime time but I thought you would be interested.

Information systems are still a "black hole" in most companies today. They remain essentially uncharted region of the enterprise while at the same time they exert a tremendous gravitational force drawing in money and resources.

The most recent analysis done in conjunction with the analysts at the Meta Group reveals some changes:

- Only 2 out of 3 companies have data on the size of their applications portfolio;
- Only 1 out of 2 companies have data on the its growth rate;
- Only 1 out of 16 have across the board data on the quality of their systems.

And with regard to the Year 2000:

- Only 1 of 3 have completed a complete impact assessment on their total portfolio.

The bad news is that it is clear that companies are not treating their systems as investments. A financial portfolio manager would be fired if he or she did not know the basics: the size of the portfolio being managed, the performance of the portfolio, and the quality and risks of the investments. A medium size company today with a portfolio of 50M lines of code essentially has an asset with a replacement cost of perhaps $500M. This is a sizable investment that is clearly not being managed as such. The financial community would not accept this, the IT community should not either.

However, these new figures are far better than those reported in previous years. This is the effect of the Year 2000 on the black hole. As Year 2000 pressure builds, companies have become acutely aware of the need to "illuminate" the black hole by increasing their quantitative knowledge of their information systems.

It appears that the black hole has a far reach too, beyond just that of the systems themselves. The results show more system-related "unknowns:"

- 34% did not have any data on their development productivity;
- 37% did not know what tools and techniques were being used in their development and support environments – not a single company had data on the depth and breadth of tool use;
- 60% did not have projections as to the distribution of work between development and maintenance for the latter part of 1997 and into 1998.

With these figures as a backdrop, let's look at where the IT dollar is going based on what we know about the black hole. Development and maintenance activities now account for about $.49 of every dollar spent. Interestingly enough, network expenses (where I've lumped in internet and intranet) now pass the data center at $.10. The "Other" category includes training and people development spending at a paltry $.03. Look at the whole picture and ask yourself a question, "How much of this money really is channeled into producing value for my enterprise?"

Now take that dollar and think about some other IT metrics. For example, in the average US company roughly 30% of maintenance costs are associated with defect removal. Is this value or non-value added work? You are correct if you pick non-value added for 7.2 cents! What about development? Figures show that up to 60% of work in many companies provides no business value at all, and that 90% of project work is rework, and that 35% of software running in production is dead code, and on and on and on …. The bottom line estimate is that an amazing $.30 of every IT dollar is non-value added. From the optimistic viewpoint, $.70 of each IT dollar gets channeled into producing business value.

Now consider where Year 2000 work fits. Most companies expect that more than $.25 of each IT dollar will now be spent on fixing that problem. I consider this to be essential but nevertheless, non-value added work. The impact of this phenomena is to further dilute the IT dollar. When the Year 2000 fully kicks in, and perhaps this is a low estimate, only $.45 of each IT dollar will be focused on producing business value. But there's more to consider.

To completely understand what IT is dealing with as we move toward the close of this millennium you must look at all the forces at work:

- Technology spending is accelerating. We are now almost 5 times the 1980s;
- The technology dollar is being diluted by its non-value added component – perhaps only $.45 contributes to generating business value.
- The $.45 doesn't buy very much because the complexity of systems and the rate of new technology introduction today has cut end-to-end productivity in half; the labor shortage has caused and will cause costs to increase.

In fact, the $.45 may only generate $.22 to $.23 in value to the enterprise because of further dilution.

Therefore, one of the "hidden" consequences of the Year 2000 problem, even if conquered, is its role in diluting the value of IT spending in the short term: 1 to 3 years.

Hidden or not hidden, the Year 2000 problem has major consequences for business worldwide. Being forewarned is key. Taking action is even more critical so you will never have to look backward at disaster.

Year 2000 Survey Results[4]

Cap Gemini has been sponsoring the collection and surveying of Year 2000 data from Fortune 500 companies by Rubin Systems Inc. for the past three years on a quarterly basis. Using the January, 1998 results, the potential GDP impact is as follows:

- The US GDP for 1996 was $7,576B. The Fortune 500 companies account for $5,077B or 67% of GDP.
- The 100 Fortune 500 companies in my latest survey account for $1,015B or 14% of GDP.
- The survey results indicate that 2 out of 3 companies in my survey do not yet have detailed plans in place to address Year 2000. That leaves $680B of the GDP unprotected, or 9% of GDP. If this sample is representative, multiply the 9% by 5 (to extrapolate for 500 companies) and that leaves 45% of the GDP unprotected.
- The survey results show that only 1 in 5 companies are in the process of executing their plan. As a result, the situation looks worse: 11% of the GDP is unprotected, and if you multiply by 5 it appears that 55% of the GDP is unprotected.
- Therefore, the only conclusion is that a *large* portion of the GDP is at risk at this time.

Here are the detailed results for the Summary of the Results of the December, 1997 Year 2000 Survey, (Sample size = 108 companies):

Key Findings

- The Year 2000 budget "pendulum" is swinging back up again. Testing, manual labor needed, and non-mainframe platform issues are the drivers.
- 77% have had to change their overall approach since starting their initiatives.

---

4   As of January, 1998.

- Cooperation and information exchange between companies and their partners/vendors is weak.
- Staffing is a big issue. Resources are scarcer than before; those doing work find it boring.
- More work is flowing back to in-house solutions while tools are not living up to their promise.
- Only 1 in 3 companies have detailed plans in place.
- End-to-end testing of all systems is a rarity in Year 2000 strategies.
- More than 88% of those surveyed do not have distinct plans to communicate their Year 2000 efforts to the public.

IT Spending

- There has been a Year 2000 spending "rebound." While companies downgraded their estimates in August 1997, there is now an increase in companies expecting to spend between 11% and 30% of their it budgets on Year 2000.
- Almost 75% of companies now think that they will be spending between 21% and 30% of their IT budget on Year 2000.
- In terms of budget allocation to the Year 2000 process, on average companies are planning the following distribution: assessment: 18%; code conversion: 22%; application level testing: 25%; suite testing: 35%.
- In terms of budget allocation for platform compliance, companies are allocating 60% of their budgets to the mainframe, 20% to the network environment, 8% to the desktop, 10% to managing their Year 2000 programs, and 2% to other system categories.
- Year 2000 is affecting both new development and maintenance by forcing reductions in these areas. Since April 1997 those deferring new development work have gone from 11% to 18% and those defer-

ring enhancements/new functionality of existing systems have grown to 30% from 22% and 25% respectively.

- Year 2000 funding is coming from predominantly outside the IT department; 25% claim to pay for it through their maintenance budgets; 40% from other IT areas; 80% from elsewhere. For the first time, 5% of companies indicate that they intend to pass through the costs to their business areas.
- Roughly 82% of companies claim they have underestimated their Year 2000 costs; only 2% are "on target" while 12% claim they are too high.

STRATEGIES/STAFFING

- Outsourcing of assessment and conversion is declining as a strategy. While 87% claimed they were doing this in April 1997, only 70% are using this strategy today.
- Conversion work appears to be moving in-house, while hybrid on-shore/off-shore approaches are on the rise. The use of off-shore resources themselves have not changed.
- The number of companies indicating a need to increase staff has risen dramatically: from 45% in April 1997 to 72% today.
- Finding staff is still classified as "difficult" by 90% of those surveyed.
- When classifying the nature of Year 2000 work, 72% of those surveyed classified it as "boring," while only 4% found it "exciting."
- The distribution of labor for companies using outside vendors is 32% internal and 68% external.

EXPERIENCES/PERCEPTION

- While 60% of companies now have completed a full assessment of their inventory, only 1 in 3 have detailed plans in place. However, 1 in 5 claim to have a full program in place.

- Regarding tools for Year 2000 support, 66% of those surveyed have found that tools do not meet their expectations, while about 24% believed they did.

- The Year 2000 issue is now the #1 priority for most IT organizations. Their priorities in dealing with the problem are ranked as speed, automation, and integrity on an equal basis.

- 90% of companies now believe that it is easier for them to assimilate tools and vendor processes than it is for vendors to learn about their systems.

CONVERSION PROFILE AND PROGRESS

- Roughly 77% of companies have changed their approach to the Year 2000 problem since they started.

- 13% of those surveyed believe that less than half of their systems will be compliant by 1/1/99, while 87% believe that more than half will be.

- The majority of companies have no standards concerning the volume of code units being passed through their processes (68%). 28% are using code blocks of 2-5 million lines of code while 4% are using less than 2 million lines of code.

- While all companies are planning to do 19xx and 20xx testing, only 60% are planning some end-to-end testing, and this is likely to be done for less than 25% of all systems.

- The level of testing completed to date is low: 35% have done 19xx, 22% have done 20xx;,and only 2% have done end-to-end.

- 38% of those surveyed have not developed contingency plans.

- The top two process issues identified are overall throughput and testing.

BUSINESS IMPACT

- The top two internal business impact areas are new product development and "time to market."
- The top two external business impact areas are customer satisfaction and delivery. Pricing impact is expected to be low.
- Business partner and vendor cooperation are ranked as somewhat poor in general.
- In terms of general impact, the impact on the stock market and banking transaction is perceived as high. Air traffic safety is ranked as very high in terms of impact.
- Most companies (more than 88% in general) have no plans to report or communicate their Year 2000 status at this time.
- Only 7% of those surveyed claim to have had a Year 2000 related failure.

Comments about Y2000 Test Certification[5]

©1998 *Paul A. Strassmann, Chairman and* CEO,
Software Testing Assurance Corporation

POLICY-MAKING executives must find new ways to obtain trusted assurance about the reliability of measures taken by computer experts on their behalf to prevent Year 2000 failures. Who will deliver assessments of the risks of business interruption? How can top management anticipate what could be charged against them as negligence if the systems organizations involved – whether they are vendors, consultants, or company employees – may be neither liable nor accountable for errors of commission or commission? Who is trustworthy if everyone involved has a potential conflict of interest in the outcome of a risk assessment that may surely lead to costly litigation?

There are precedents for creating trusted and independent institutions that would offer expert certification attesting that what is alleged is indeed true. For instance, the concerns about the reliability of accounting records has led to the formation of auditing firms that will certify compliance of financial accounts with generally accepted standards. There are materials testing laboratories that attest the adherence of steel and concrete samples to industry-sanctioned specifications. The conformity of articles of commerce with generally accepted standards was seen to be of sufficient importance to merit a reference to standards for weights and measures in the Constitution of the United States.

As the economy of advanced societies increasingly relies exclusively on transactions created, supported, and conveyed by software it becomes imperative to find new ways to assure everyone involved of the reliability and trustworthiness of electronically transmitted data. That calls for standards that would define the criteria for judging what

5 The methods and ideas in this section do not necessarily represent the views of the other authors of this book, their employers, or other organizations with which they may be affiliated.

are trusted software-based processes. That makes it necessary to create institutions that would be accountable for delivering independently verifiable attestations about conformity of software with publicly promulgated and generally accepted testing standards.

The assessors of Y2000 liabilities will need exceptional technological know-how and verification tools to come up with independent evaluations that can be backed by insurance. Amid the confusion about the soundness of conflicting technological claims, corporate executives will surely find it comforting to obtain independent checks of the validity of the vendors' claims as long as there is a public standard against which to compare facts against allegations.

Information services assessment enterprises will become the growth sector of the consulting business. Such groups may end up as the underwriters of technology risks arising from poorly functioning software. The reliance on independent certification of software becomes especially critical for all firms that have divested themselves of an independent capacity to make judgments about their computer investments. Such a condition would be especially acute in cases where outsourcing of their information technologies to service companies or shifting total reliance on software designed and maintained by software firms increases the dependency on others. The new assessors may therefore evolve and become the risk insurers against technological and economic disasters that nowadays are endemic to the poor software management practices that are present in virtually all organizations.

INITIATING A TESTING CERTIFICATION STANDARD

To LIMIT the risks of Year 2000 failures, the Software Testing Assurance Corporation engaged professionally recognized specialists in testing of software to draft a Y2000 Testing Certification Standard. At a meeting of some of the most renowned software experts held January 29, 1998 at the Software Productivity Consortium, the proposed standard was discussed and transferred to the public domain for further processing as a proposed industry standard. These steps are seen as the start of a concerted long-term effort to establish an independent software certification capability in the USA.

I believe that the readers of this volume, which is dedicated to the evaluation of a company's chances of Year 2000 project success, can gain from an inclusion of the proposed standard as a reference against which further work must be done. The proposed standard covers more testing issues than have been addressed in the prior pages and therefore can serve as an additional detailed checklist of what it would take to gain further assurances that Year 2000 tasks will be successfully completed.

A Y2000 Testing Certification Standard[6]

Scope

This document establishes criteria for evaluating the effectiveness of software testing performed for the purpose of finding Year 2000 related problems. Software testing in this document includes all activities intended to find problems in software (e.g. structured walkthroughs, inspections, static analysis techniques, executed program testing, and formal techniques to find problems during requirements analysis and design). Evaluation will require an examiner to weigh the level of software risk to the enterprise against the software testing techniques chosen to mitigate the risk. An examination will require evidence of analysis of risk from software failures; those failures from Year 2000 date problems.

This document, then, provides the criteria needed determine if the software testing techniques are likely to be adequate to mitigate the risks. No testing process guarantees zero defects in software. Thus there always remains a risk of a software failure with possible business or human consequences. However, there is strong evidence that certain software test techniques are more effective at finding problems. The criteria given in this document represents those deemed effective by its authors and reviewers. It must be noted that these criteria emphasize the need for thorough analysis of each certification situation. Further, these criteria, in and of themselves, do not guarantee against Y2K defects. It remains the responsibility of the enterprise to make the final determination of what constitutes complete and adequate testing.

In the discussion of any process, consideration must be given to three elements. First, is the "standard," which is the reference for determining that the effort has been successful. Second are the "best practices" which describe the most effective means of conducting the effort. Third is the "assessment" which measures whether or not the product meets the standard.

This document will focus exclusively on defining the standard for certification of software to meet Y2K compliance. In particular, the standard described here is limited to the standards necessary for assurance that software is Y2K compliant, that is, the testing requirements. This document does not address other possible Y2K standards such as remediation techniques or configuration management.

In this certification standard, assurance that software is Y2K compliant is approached from a "business risk" viewpoint. The level of assurance required to obtain certification will be based on the impact of a Y2K failure on the enterprise where it is used. To this end, the certification criteria described in this standard are organized into two parts. First are criteria for evaluation of the business impact of a Y2K failure of software employed in the enterprise.

Second are the criteria for analysis and execution of the software testing necessary to ensure that the software will not pose unacceptable risk to the enterprise due to a Y2K defect. The document also addresses the application of automated tools to support the test process.

This document is sufficiently detailed such that the user can reliably assess risks associated with Y2K defects and derive an adequate testing strategy. It is also broad enough so it can be used across a range of software applications (flight control, financial management, operating systems) and client applications (software vendors, in-house development, contract programming).

Establishment of a Y2K standard assumes an assessment will be made to determine whether or not the standard has been or will be met. Therefore, an overarching requirement for all aspects of the certification is that:

- The enterprise fulfills the requirements of the standard;
- There exists sufficient documentation to determine that the standard was, or will be attained.

RELATIONSHIP TO OTHER STANDARDS

OTHER EFFORTS have been made or are underway to describe the processes and practices for software engineering (i.e., development), in general, and for Year 2000 testing, in particular. This document does not attempt to reproduce or replace these efforts. For example the Carnegie Mellon Software Engineering Institute's Capability Maturity Model provides a solid process framework for organizations and individuals to follow in performing software development and testing. Standards bodies, such as NIST and IEEE, have prepared, or are preparing, recommendations for the Year 2000 testing practice. Industry groups are also making available materials to address specific aspects of Y2K remediation and testing.

This document differs from these others in that it focuses on the linkage between Y2K software remediation and the business risks associated with defects that may occur during that remediation.

DEFINITION OF TERMS

To AID comprehension and ensure continuity within this document, the following terms are defined:

- **Software system:** A collection of programs, databases or files, and documentation which accomplish a defined set of functions.
- **Software component:** Any one of the programs, modules, files, or other parts of the software system.
- **Testing:** Any process used to confirm a characteristic of a software system or component. For Y2K certification purposes, inspections, walkthroughs and actual execution of software are all examples of testing.

Document Organization

THE CERTIFICATION requirements are addressed in three titles, each focusing on a major component of the certification criteria.

Title 1 describes the certification criteria associated with assessment of business risk and software system criticality. To meet the requirements of this title, the enterprise establishes the role of the software in the business enterprise to be certified and the risks that this software poses if Y2K defects are discovered during its intended use. The information developed in this title will define and justify the level of testing called out in the next title.

Title 2 defines the required characteristics that will constitute an adequate test of the software system, based on business risk:

- **Test approach:** How the testing will be accomplished.
- **Component inventory:** What software will be tested.
- **Test completion criteria:** What the test goals are.
- **Test case design:** How the test cases are specified.
- **Test case implementation:** Construction and execution of the test cases.
- **Test verification:** Confirmation that ex-pected results and completion criteria are met.

Title 3 assesses the tools used to assist the design, planning, management, and execution of the test effort. Its purpose is to discover whether or not the tools support the tests or if reliance on a particular tool introduces the potential for missing defects in the software.

Title 1: Software Criticality Analysis

As a practical matter, the level of effort devoted to testing should reflect the importance of the software to the enterprise that maintains or uses it. Software critical to the enterprise must undergo more stringent testing than software that plays a lesser role. For example, establishing that a software system is used in mission-critical situations would dictate very stringent test criteria and assurance that these criteria were met. On the other hand, an examiner's assessment that the target software plays only an incidental role in the ability of the organization to perform its functions would change the nature of the risk exposure and of the test requirements to minimize that exposure.

Without a clear assessment of a software system's business criticality, there is no sound basis for assigning technical testing criteria. Therefore, this standard requires an effective analysis of the business risks posed by a Y2K failure in a software component and the remediation/test effort. The required analysis has two elements, each with criteria to be met in order to be in compliance with the standard:

Software System Assessment

Criteria: All software systems used in the business enterprise and which are intended to be certified must be clearly identified and the impact of Y2K determined.

Discussion: The software that will be subject to the Y2K Test Certification must be clearly specified. The software system assessment must include the following:

All software systems employed in the enterprise must be identified. This includes in-house and vendor supplied systems. It also encompasses applications, operating systems, utilities (e.g. database engines, sort/merge packages), and embedded systems. If the enterprise utilizes outside agents, then all software systems used by the agent to deliver the functionality, product, or service must be identified. This identification of systems must be sufficiently complete such that the exact configuration is unambiguous as remediation and test work goes forward.

There must be a mapping of the software system products and functions to the business functions, products, and services. The level of mapping detail is dictated by the variety of business functions in which the software system is involved and the criticality of each function to the business. For example, if virtually all of the system's functionality and products support a single business area, then it is sufficient to map the entire system to the major business functions conducted in that area. If, however, the software system supports diverse business functions of varying importance, then specific software system components and products must be mapped to the specific business components that they support. For example, if two reports out of a financial system are critical to meeting a customer order while the remaining system products are less consequential, then those reports and their associated software components must be identified.

Interrelations between software systems must also be clearly identified. For example, applications should be tied to the operating systems on which they execute, the utilities which support them, and the systems from which they receive and to which they provide data.

An assessment of the date-sensitivity of each software system is required. This assessment must be as quantitative as possible and provide a clear assessment of the importance of date processing to the functionality of the system. The specific method of assessment will depend on the nature of the software system and the tools available. For example, it could be based on automated count and categorization of the number of lines of code with date logic or the number of functions utilizing a date sensitive algorithm.

Business Risk Assignment

Criteria: Each software system subject to certification must be rated as to the risk posed to the business should that system or its components fail due to a Y2K defect.

Discussion: Having identified the scope of the business entity and mapped the supporting software systems, a risk assessment must be produced. At the completion of this effort, there must be a clear assignment of criticality to each software system and its subcomponents upon which technical remediation and testing requirements can be built. There must be process documentation and an audit trail of the risk decisions such that an examiner can understand and evaluate how a software component was assigned a given criticality (and subsequently required to meet defined test completion criteria).

The techniques and technology for risk assessment are beyond the scope of this document. Whatever methodology is employed, the risk assignment must incorporate the following elements:

- For all business functions supported by software, the criticality of that function to the success of the overall business must be rated. This classification should be of a granularity that supports clear understanding of the impact of a failure on the business as a whole and allows for useful gradations of test requirements. For example, business criticality might be divided into the following categories:

- Function is absolutely essential to the business; must be available for each business day. Failure of function puts customer base or financial viability at immediate and significant risk.
- Function is important but not essential; business and customer base can operate without it for a short period of time. Customer and financial impact can be mitigated.
- Function necessary for organization to operate in an efficient fashion.
- Non-availability does not affect customers or financial viability, however efficiency, flexibility and effectiveness of the enterprise are impacted.

Where the business function is mapped to a software system, the impact of a Y2K failure of that software component on the business entity must be assessed. This assessment should be as quantitative as possible. In any case, the assessment should be structured such that specific test completion criteria can be assigned that are appropriate to the business risks.

Examples of software criticality classifications that might be used include:

- Business function can operate for a while without the availability of the software system, however effectiveness and efficiency of the function is significantly degraded.
- Business function is highly or totally dependent on reliable and correct operation of the software system.
- Business function can employ work-arounds and operate indefinitely without the software system; only the efficiency of the business process is impacted.

The risk assignment must factor the ability of contingency, work-around, and recovery procedures to mitigate the impact of a Y2K defect on the business. The risk assessment must also factor the extent of the remediation and test effort into the risk. If remediation and testing cannot be completed before Y2K dates begin entering the system, then a higher risk of business impact must be assigned.

The risk assessment must bring the elements defined above together and produce a final rating that can be used to assign appropriate test certification criteria to each software system or component. The exact rating system is discretionary, however it must be such that there is unambiguous linkage to the test criteria.

An example of a rating approach might be assignment of software to one of four categories:

- Software is essential to one or more critical business functions. It must be tested to a level that makes the likelihood of a Y2K failure virtually non-existent.
- Software is important to non-critical business functions and recovery from errors requires effort but is possible. It must be tested to a level of reliability equivalent to other maintenance changes.
- Software system or business function is not essential to business survival and adequate system support staff is available. Software must be tested to a level that provides assurances that all date decisions are made correctly.
- Defects in date formatting are acceptable.

TITLE 2: TEST CERTIFICATION CRITERIA

TITLE 1 established a clear relationship between the software system requiring certification and the risks that a Y2K failure in the system would pose to the business. Testing of the software seeks to mitigate that risk by detecting defects in the remediation of the code that would cause the software to not process dates correctly. The characteristics of the test process determine the level of confidence that the enterprise has in the software's likelihood of correct behavior. This confidence factor, in turn, defines the actual risk of a business interruption or loss when the system is re-implemented.

The Y2K Test Certification requires clear evidence that the testing effort is designed to assure Y2K compliance at the appropriate risk level. The elements of this demonstration are described below:

Testing Approach

Criteria: Testing of systems for Y2K compliance must be done in the context of a defined test strategy. The strategy must specify how testing will be accomplished. The strategy must be consistent with and clearly effective in mitigating the level of business risk posed by the software.

Discussion: The test strategy for each risk category must be clearly delineated. The strategy must detail the types of testing that will be done, the sources of test cases and test data, description of the test execution environment, and other elements that will be required for the tests to go successfully. It also outlines the processes that will be followed to design, build, and execute the tests. The strategy must be comprehensive and of sufficient detail that adherence can be validated throughout the testing effort.

To the extent that different test approaches are applied to different systems or levels of business risk, the strategy must provide a clear process for assigning the correct approach to the appropriate software system or component.

Test Completion Criteria

Criteria: All testing must be based on attainment of quantitative test completion goals in the design and execution of test cases. The selected goals must be consistent with the characteristics of the software system and the types of Y2K defects, which may exist.

Discussion: Many organizations define testing as exercising the code until the project runs out of time and resources. Testers throw tests at cycle after cycle hoping that defects will be discovered. The effort has no agreed upon and quantifiable criteria for saying that testing is completed. The test effort is non-directed. The true quality of the system is not known until it has been running in production.

Y2K certification will require directed testing. In directed testing, testers have specific, quantifiable goals. It is agreed that testing is completed when the goals have been reached. There must be quantifiable test criteria based on the business risk posed by a Y2K failure of the software system.

To meet the Y2K test certification standard, the software system must be tested against quantitative test completion criteria which reflect the business criticality of the software and thus the level of risk that is to be mitigated by the testing. These criteria and a clear description of their implementation must be clearly defined.

No single test completion criterion will catch all defects. Each criterion imposes time effort and cost on the test effort. Y2K test certification will require that a set of test criteria be selected based on the following:

- The criteria are quantifiable, allowing progress towards completion to be measured.
- The criteria have a demonstrated history or sound technical rationale of detecting defects.
- The test organization has the tools and capability to design and execute tests based on the selected criteria.

Quantitative completion criteria include, but are not limited to technical coverage techniques such as code coverage or functional variation coverage.

Other types of test goals should also be considered. A defined process for date warps is a valid and necessary Y2K test completion criterion, as is execution of the software against specific dates of business significance (e.g., last day of quarter and month). Other examples of quantitative test criteria are listed in Addendum C. In addition, different sets of criteria can be established based on varying levels of business criticality or differing characteristics of the systems under test. Code coverage may be appropriate for COBOL programs, but impossible for assembler modules. Requiring only one date warp might be considered sufficient for non-critical reporting systems, however, multiple date warps of specified intervals would be more appropriate for critical file-update applications.

Whatever criteria are chosen, there must be a clear demonstration that they are appropriate to the technical attributes of the software and will be sufficient to mitigate the risk of subsequent (post-test) failure.

Technical Test Inventory

Criteria: There must be a complete inventory of the software components that are to undergo testing.

Discussion: The test process must develop a clear inventory of the software components that are subject to Y2K testing. This inventory differs from the Y2K impact assessment done as part of the risk assignment in Title 1. Here the specific software components are inventoried to ensure that they are included in the testing effort.

What is inventoried depends upon the test approach and test completion criteria. If extensive code coverage or other white-box testing is planned, then all date-sensitive lines of code must be identified. If a test criterion is execution of the system on all critical business dates, then a complete list of the required dates, cross-referenced to the systems that use them, is necessary.

For test completion criteria such as date warps, the inventory should list the components that require warping. As part of the documentation of the inventory, the processes and tools used to create the inventory must also be specified. Examples of inventory approaches are given in Addendum B of this standard.

Test Case Design

Criteria: The test case design must enumerate inputs and expected results for each test case. The tests must be designed to meet the completion criteria.

Discussion: Test case design is the process of specifying a set of beginning and ending states of a software system and the execution circumstances (data, execution sequence, etc.) that will achieve the desired test completion criteria. For Y2K certification, the process of test case design must be clearly documented. This documentation must include:

- A description of the design processes, including demonstration of how the resulting test case designs meet one or more of the test completion criteria.

- Documentation of the test case designs. For each test case, the inputs and expected outputs of the test must be delineated.
- Notation of all situations where it is not practical or feasible to design test cases to meet a criterion. For example, a test design that requires dropping power on the mainframe.

Y2K certification of the test design will be based on an assessment that the test design processes and the resulting test cases will fulfill the test completion criteria. For critical systems, it would be expected that the design process will be more rigorous that for non-critical systems. For example, designing tests for full date warp coverage in a critical system should include processes of code and data analysis that explicitly define the dates needed for each date decision or computation. In less critical systems, test case design based on a set of standard date progressions (i.e., advance the date in three 14-day increments starting with December 15, 1999) might be more appropriate.

Implementation

Criteria: Test cases must be implemented according to the test design specification and executed in a fashion that ensures they meet the design and coverage requirements.

Discussion: Test implementation refers to the construction of test data and executable test scripts, followed by execution of the scripts and retention of test results. For test certification, implementation must ensure that the test cases, as executed, reflect the test case design. A certified test case implementation will contain the following elements:

- Direct traceability between the test case design specifications and the actual test scripts, data values and expected results.
- Clear description of the test execution process.
- Verification that all the test cases are executed at least once and the results obtained.
- Retesting is done as problems are fixed.
- Notation of all situations or anomalies that either precluded execution of tests or affect the results.

Verification

Criteria: Verification must confirm that 1) the test results match the expected results, and 2) the test completion criteria and business risk mitigation goals have been met.

Discussion: Certification requires that, as a result of the design and implementation of test cases, there be positive and complete demonstration that test completion criteria are met and that the software system provided the expected results.

While there are no specific documentation formats required, the documentation offered for examination must provide the following:

- Definition of the techniques employed to conduct verification. The means by which verification is done will vary with the nature of the software system, the availability of tools and the business criticality of the software component. For example, verification of code coverage in a critical software component would require use of a code coverage monitor (presuming one exists for the language). In a less critical software component, verification of coverage would require manually walking the test cases through the code. More extensive examples of verification options are shown in Addendum D.
- Documentation showing that the software system behaved as expected for each test.
- Documentation clearly showing the extent to which the test completion criteria were achieved, plus any mitigating circumstances or known problems.
- Documentation of any anomalies in the test results, which prevent full and complete verification of the tests.

Title 3: Evaluation of Tools Used in Test Process

THE TESTING of any non-trivial software system involves considerable human resources and the evaluation of significant amounts of information. Test cases must be designed. Test data must be built. Tests will be executed and the results evaluated multiple times in the course of the test effort. Many of these activities lend themselves to the use of automated tools to perform specific testing functions such as automatic execution of cases, validation of results and design of the test cases.

Tools ease the test burden and improve the process as they perform their functions more reliably than an equivalent manual effort. However, to the extent that the test process depends on tools to perform critical test functions, the reliability and efficacy of the tools must be examined as part of any software assurance or indemnification evaluation.

Where tools are employed to assist testing, these tools will be subject to examination as part of the overall test evaluation process. Specific questions will be developed to profile the following topics:

- Profile software or hardware tool support used in the process of testing, its management, or documentation of results. Identify all such tools and what their roles are in the test process.
- Characterize the criticality of the role played by each tool in the specific test process under examination. Does the tool provide assistance to an otherwise manual test process, or is the tool relied upon to perform a test process with little or no human oversight? For example, a word processor used to document test results is less critical than hardware used to test imbedded software.
- Evaluate the ability of the test team to detect a failure of the test tool to perform its function.
- Determine if there are industry or regulatory certification criteria for the type test tool and whether or not the specific tool has obtained that certification.
- Evaluate whether the tool was applied appropriately to this particular software test effort and environment.
- Evaluate whether the test activity performed by the tool was the activity intended by the tester. For

example, do the validation criteria implemented by the tool match the criteria intended by the tester?
• Characterize the knowledge and experience of the test team in using the tool.

ADDENDUM A

THE FOLLOWING are examples of detailed technical impact assessments that might be required to fully define the software system components that must be tested.

Breakout the software system into its subcomponents to a level of detail that allows varying assignment of test criteria based on the specific business risk posed by that subcomponent. For example, the main re-order subsystem of an inventory application would be broken out from the history reporting subsystem since the former is more critical to the business and thus must be tested to a higher certification standard:
• Identification of each data element used in the software component, which may hold a date value. "Used" means data elements that are accepted into, generated out of, or employed in the logic of the software.
• Identification of all instances where a software component utilizes a date value of special significance. "Special significance" includes reserved dates (dates used as codes) and dates that have special business meaning (e.g., month end, quarter end, year end) and dates with special meaning to the software component (e.g., day of the week, ordinal date, leap year).
• Identification of all instances where the chosen remediation solution results in changes to data structures such that a software component can misinterpret the value of the data element, whether it is used internally or at the component interface, and that all such data elements have been identified. For example, expansion of a date

field in the data structure of a flat file will change the displacement of subsequent data elements. If those elements are used by a software component, then that relationship must have been identified.
- Identification of all interfaces containing dates for each software system component.
- Identification of all functions contained in the software system which utilize dates in decisions or computations. This identification may be based on examination of code, direct observation of the system's behavior, or analysis of functional specifications.

If the remediation method changes the external functional behavior of the component, then all new functions and software components must be identified.

Addendum B

Identification of code requiring remediation and testing:

- Identification of all code contained in production code management libraries.
- Review of code inventory by business and technical staff knowledgeable of the application.
- Reconciliation of all inputs and outputs to each software component to ensure that all interfaces have been identified and considered for remediation and testing.
- Review of production logs for evidence of code that was run but is managed outside of the standard code management environment.
- Rules or rationale for excluding specific programs or modules.

Identification of date-impacted code:

- Employment of a standard commercial list of identifiers. For example, data elements with "DT," "YY" in the data element name.
- Knowledgeable application experts review and augment the starting list of date identifiers.
- All data elements which potentially can receive a date, whether or not they qualify from the original identification list, are included in the marking of date-impacted code.
- The method of identification captures and stores information about the context in which the data elements are used in the code (e.g., comparisons or calculations).
- Data structure aliases are included in the marking of date-impacted code.
- This includes identification of parent-child data relationships.
- When an identifier is removed from the list, the rationale for its removal is documented.
- Data stores are examined to identify and/or confirm the existence of data elements containing date values.
- Identification of reserve dates and dates of special significance.
- Examination of all date-impacted code involving a decision where the decision utilizes a constant value or employs a table of dates.
- Use of an industry standard list of reserved dates.
- Review of software application functionality by subject matter experts for their knowledge of special significance dates.
- Confirmation of list of special dates as provided by the subject matter experts via examination of the code.
- Production scheduling and execution logs are examined to identify cyclical executions of soft-

ware components based on calendar periods (i.e., end-of-month).

Identification of modified data structures:

- Explicit examination of all data structures and clear identification of all data elements that are displaced or modified as part of remediation.
- Cross reference of data structures to software components confirming the impact of the change on each software component.
- Examination of actual test results (regardless of whether the data structures were evaluated prior to test).

Identification of all interfaces:

- All input and output data structures for each component were identified.
- The software component(s) responsible for supplying the data to this component were identified. The software component(s) receiving the outputs of this component were identified.
- Interface identification was limited to identification of data stores and the components that interact with them.
- Interfaces were not identified, however, an integrated test of all software components was executed.

ADDENDUM C

Code and branch coverage: Testing will execute, at least once, all software code instructions that assign or use date values in the data elements identified in the test requirements. In addition, where the instruction represents a decision branch based on a date value, all branch vectors must have been executed at least once. Code coverage criteria can be applied to the source code, or if source level coverage is not possible or practical, coverage may be applied at the generated code level.

Functional coverage: Testing will execute each functional variation associated with functions that contain date logic or date transformation. Functional coverage requires complete and unambiguous specification of the functional logic, either from specifications or some form of reverse engineering of the software.

Data path coverage: Testing will exercise each data set-use path in the code that is considered Y2K date sensitive.

Trusted regression coverage: The library of regression test cases has a demonstrated history of defect detection such that the software system exhibits high reliability once it has passed the regression test suite.

An additional Y2K-specific category of test criteria is date warping. The following criteria must be considered:

- Where source code instructions compare a date to a constant or assign, reference, or copy a date, the test coverage must ensure that date values prior to and following 12/31/1999 were used.
- Where source code instructions involve an explicit or implicit comparison of dates or date computation (e.g,. DATE2 set to DATE1 + 30 days), the coverage must ensure that date values are used such that the comparison range is a) completely in this century, b) completely in the next century, and c) spans the century boundary (e.g., DATE1 is in century '19' and DATE2 is in century '20').
- Recurring dates of special significance to functionality of the software component (e.g. end-of-month) are correctly processed for date values prior to and after 12/31/1999. All reserve dates of significance to the software component have been exercised.
- Test cases confirm that the passing of all dates between software components remains consistent and correct.

ADDENDUM D

SAMPLE VERIFICATION techniques for code coverage, date warping, and other test criteria:

Code Coverage: Evaluate the extent to which attainment and verification of code coverage was achieved. Which of the following techniques were applied:

- All executable code was explicitly instrumented and coverage is reported.
- Test results are consistent with expected results.
- Test cases executed were specifically designed to traverse the code identified as having a date impact, however the code itself is not instrumented and thus coverage cannot be confirmed.
- A suite of regression test cases was executed for which the overall code coverage is known, but for which date-sensitive coverage is not known.
- Code was not instrumented to validate coverage of date-sensitive instructions.
- A test design or execution technique is utilized which traditionally provides very high coverage and yields consistent reliability. Coverage is not verified.
- Code coverage is accomplished through execution of only the date-related instructions using debugging or interpretive tools. Component as a whole is not tested.
- Test cases derived from or representing typical usage of the software component are executed. Coverage is not verified.
- Test cases are developed based on experience and judgment of the test team.
- Code is remediated and placed back into its intended environment. Defects are handled as they arise.

Execution of date ranges: Evaluate the adequacy of testing across date values. Which of the following techniques are employed:

- Values assigned in test data are explicitly checked against their usage in the code. Each usage has explicit test values that meet criteria for date ranges.
- A set of test data is developed which meets "current century requirements."
- The data is then subject to multiple iterations of "aging" and executed during test. There is no confirmation that all aging criteria have been met for each date usage in the software component.
- No aging or significant value testing is done. Testing does confirm that code continues to work correctly in current millennium.

Interface coverage: Evaluate the extent to which component interfaces have been tested to ensure proper communication of date values. Which of the following techniques are used:

- Test cases are developed for interfaces to demonstrate that both components interpret the date information correctly – where both components use the date as a date value both interpret it as the same date.
- Test cases and results show that where both components use the date as a reserved date both components interpret the meaning in the same way.
- Testing of a software component was done against the specification of interface requirements for the other component rather than execution of the component itself.
- Code coverage test cases are employed and interfaces are observed to work correctly; no explicit exercising of cross-component date functionality is done.

Functional Variations: Evaluate the extent to which new and changed functionality has been tested to assure correct behavior. Which of the following techniques are used:

- Functional test cases derived from a written specification and exercising all functional variations are executed.

- Full code coverage was achieved in the testing of this component.
- No specific test completion criteria were utilized, however, this functionality was included in the overall testing of the application.

For More Information

Name: _____ Title: _____

Organization:_____

Address: _____

City: _____ State: _____

Zip Code: _____ Country: _____

Telephone: _____ Fax:_____

❑ Please send me information on obtaining licensing rights to Year
2000 **QuickSTATus.**

❑ Please send me information about the Year 2000 **QuickSTATus
Analysis Toolset.**

❑ Please send me ___ additional copies of Year 2000 **QuickSTATus**
for $24.95 each (enclose payment).

❑ Please send me ___ copies of *The Year 2000 Planning Guide* for
$295.00 each (enclose payment).

Mail or fax this form to:
   Rubin Systems, Inc.
   PO Box 387
   Pound Ridge, NY 10576
   Fax: 914-764-0536

The Year 2000 **QuickSTATus** methodology was developed by
Rubin Systems, Inc.

Rubin Systems, Inc.
PO Box 387
Pound Ridge, NY 10576

CONTACT INFORMATION:

Rubin Systems, Inc.
PO Box 387
Pound Ridge, NY 10576
Fax: 914-764-0536
Email: howard_rubin@compuserve.com

Visit the Rubin Systems, Inc. web site: www.hrubin.com